D1540604

The Art of Lean Software Development

Other resources from O'Reilly

Related titles

Head First Software
Development

The Art of Agile
Development

Java Extreme
Programming
Cookbook™

Beautiful Code

Head First Design Patte

Extreme Programming
Pocket Guide

NUnit Pocket Reference

JUnit Pocket Guide

oreilly.com

oreilly.com is more than a complete catalog of O'R
books. You'll also find links to news, events, arti
weblogs, sample chapters, and code examples.

oreillynet.com is the essential portal for developers intere
in open and emerging technologies, including new p
forms, programming languages, and operating systems

Conferences

O'Reilly brings diverse innovators together to nurture
ideas that spark revolutionary industries. We specializ
documenting the latest tools and systems, translating
innovator's knowledge into useful skills for those in
trenches. Visit *conferences.oreilly.com* for our upcom
events.

Safari Bookshelf (*safari.oreilly.com*) is the premier on
reference library for programmers and IT profession
Conduct searches across more than 1,000 books. S
scribers can zero in on answers to time-critical questi
in a matter of seconds. Read the books on your Books
from cover to cover or simply flip to the page you n
Try it today for free.

The Art of Lean Software Development

Development

Curt Hibbs, Steve Jewett, and Mike Sullivan

The Art of Lean Software Development
by Curt Hibbs, Steve Jewett, and Mike Sullivan

Copyright © 2009 Curt Hibbs, Stephen Jewett, and Mike Sullivan. All rights reserved.
Printed in the United States of America.

Published by O'Reilly Media, Inc., 1005 Gravenstein Highway North, Sebastopol, CA 95472.

O'Reilly books may be purchased for educational, business, or sales promotional use. Online editions are also available for most titles (*http://safari.oreilly.com*). For more information, contact our corporate/institutional sales department: 800-998-9938 or *corporate@oreilly.com*.

Editor: Mike Loukides
Production Editor: Sarah Schneider
Copyeditor: Amy Thomson
Proofreader: Kiel Van Horn

Indexer: Fred Brown
Cover Designer: Monica Kamsvaag
Interior Designer: Marcia Friedman
Illustrator: Jessamyn Read
Photographer: Mike Sullivan

Printing History:

December 2008: First Edition.

O'Reilly and the O'Reilly logo are registered trademarks of O'Reilly Media, Inc. *The Art of Lean Software Development*, the image of a kite, and related trade dress are trademarks of O'Reilly Media, Inc.

Many of the designations used by manufacturers and sellers to distinguish their products are claimed as trademarks. Where those designations appear in this book, and O'Reilly Media, Inc. was aware of a trademark claim, the designations have been printed in caps or initial caps.

While every precaution has been taken in the preparation of this book, the publisher and authors assume no responsibility for errors or omissions, or for damages resulting from the use of the information contained herein.

ISBN: 978-0-596-51731-1

[V]

1231794476

CONTENTS

PREFACE

The most valuable of all talents is that of never using two words when one will do.

—Thomas Jefferson

Everything has a beginning.

Sometimes you can point to a single event that set the wheels in motion, whereas other times a soup of ideas, events, and thoughts coagulate in some mysterious way that we never fully comprehend. In the case of this book, the "single event" model definitely applies.

Curt remembers it like it was yesterday—the first time he sat down with a colleague to discuss Lean software development. As they discussed what Lean thinking meant when applied to software development, the colleague asked one simple question: "If I could do only one thing, what should that be?"

It was a good question, a question that stuck in Curt's mind like a song that you can't stop hearing in your head, over and over. Pondering this question led him to better understand how much software developers and managers really *want* to believe that this Lean and Agile development stuff can help them. They feel like they ought to do something, but they're reluctant (or unable) to adopt a whole methodology because of a legitimate fear of failure.

It's like asking someone to jump off a cliff with a handy-dandy new jet pack strapped to his back, saying, "Trust me, this will get you to the other side of that chasm much faster." Maybe… but what are the consequences if it doesn't work?

If that's how you feel, this book is for you.

The Lean approach has been yielding dramatic results in manufacturing for decades, and now Lean is being applied just as successfully to the supply chain, product design, engineering, and even software development! At the same time, the Agile software development methodologies have been proving the value of the very same core practices recommended for Lean software development.

These core practices are common to every Agile methodology and Lean software development implementation. Best of all, these practices can be adopted one at a time and still provide substantial benefits—you don't have to swallow the elephant whole to see benefits.

Many people mistakenly think that Lean and Agile are two names for the same thing. Lean and Agile software development have the same goal—to increase quality and productivity—but they take different philosophical approaches to get there. The first part of this book presents the Lean software development principles. We discuss the differences between the Lean and Agile perspectives as well as the similarities.

The second part of this book presents the core practices, ordered by value. We tell you which practice you should use first to get the most return for your effort and, if you are already doing that, we show you which practice you should adopt next.

This book covers, in detail, the five most important practices that you can adopt as you begin your Lean software development journey. These are simple, incremental steps you can take to lean out your software development—one step at a time!

As you master each practice, you will see significant, measurable results. These successes will give you a deeper understanding of the power of applying Lean thinking to software development.

The more improvements you make to your software development process, the more attuned you will become to the impediments that still exist ("waste," in Lean terms). This will give you the knowledge and ability to start making your own value judgments about how to continue improving your software development process. After all, Lean is a journey, not a destination!

Who Should Read This Book?

This book is for software developers and managers of software developers who are new to Lean software development and, possibly, new to Agile software development. It is for those who want to quickly understand why Lean software development is important and what it can do for you.

This is purposefully a short book, with short chapters. We know that you are just as busy as we are, and we don't believe in padding our chapters with useless fluff. In every chapter we try to be as succinct and to-the-point as possible. Our goal is to introduce you to the important topics and resources so that you know where to go when you need more details.

Conventions Used in This Book

The following typographical conventions are used in this book:

Italic

    Indicates new terms, URLs, email addresses, filenames, and file extensions.

`Constant width`

    Indicates computer code in a broad sense, including commands, options, switches, variables, attributes, keys, functions, types, classes, namespaces, methods, modules, properties, parameters, values, objects, events, event handlers, XML tags, HTML tags, macros, the contents of files, and the output from the commands.

Using Code Examples

This book is here to help you get your job done. In general, you may use the code in this book in your programs and documentation. You do not need to contact us for permission unless you're reproducing a significant portion of the code. For example, writing a program that uses several chunks of code from this book does not require permission. Selling or distributing a CD-ROM of examples from O'Reilly books does require permission. Answering a question by citing this book and quoting example code does not require permission. Incorporating a significant amount of example code from this book into your product's documentation does require permission.

We appreciate, but do not require, attribution. An attribution usually includes the title, author, publisher, and ISBN. For example, "*The Art of Lean Software Development* by Curt Hibbs, Steve Jewett, and Mike Sullivan. Copyright 2009 Curt Hibbs, Stephen Jewett, and Mike Sullivan, 978-0-596-51731-1."

If you feel your use of code examples falls outside fair use or the permission given above, feel free to contact us at *permissions@oreilly.com*.

Safari® Books Online

Safari   When you see a Safari® Books Online icon on the cover of your favorite technology book, that means the book is available online through the O'Reilly Network Safari Bookshelf.

Safari offers a solution that's better than e-books. It's a virtual library that lets you easily search thousands of top tech books, cut and paste code samples, download chapters, and find quick answers when you need the most accurate, current information. Try it for free at *http://safari .oreilly.com*.

Comments and Questions

Please address comments and questions concerning this book to the publisher:

O'Reilly Media, Inc.
1005 Gravenstein Highway North
Sebastopol, CA 95472
800-998-9938 (in the United States or Canada)
707-829-0515 (international or local)
707-829-0104 (fax)

We have a web page for this book where we list errata, examples, and any additional information. You can access this page at:

http://oreilly.com/catalog/9780596517311/

To comment or ask technical questions about this book, send email to:

bookquestions@oreilly.com

For more information about our books, conferences, Resource Centers, and the O'Reilly Network, see our website at:

http://www.oreilly.com

Acknowledgments

We would be remiss if we did not thank all of the people who helped make this book a reality. This includes the good people at O'Reilly who believed this book was worth publishing, and our families who let us disappear behind closed doors to write it.

We'd also like to thank the early reviewers whose feedback made this a better book: Kelly Carter, Ted Davis, Laurent Julliard, John McClenning, Phyllis Marbach, Bill Niebruegge, Ian Roth, Beth Simon, Tim Sullivan, Ed Thoms, and Brian Wells.

But most of all, we'd like to thank Beth Simon for asking that one simple question!

CHAPTER ONE

Why Lean?

Optimism is an occupational hazard of programming.

—Kent Beck

The practice of software development has been plagued with shockingly low success rates for decades. At the same time, the number of software-driven products and services continues to increase dramatically each year. If these were the only two trends, we would be heading for disaster.

Fortunately, Agile software development methods have been demonstrating that higher success rates are possible. And Lean techniques (which have dramatically increased manufacturing success for over 50 years) are now being applied to software development and validating the successes of Agile.

The Lean principles and the mindset of Lean thinking have proved remarkably applicable to improving the productivity and quality of just about any endeavor. Lean has been successfully applied to manufacturing, distribution, supply chain, product development, banking, engineering, the back office, and much more. However, only in the last few years have the Lean principles and techniques been applied to software development.

In this chapter we will give you more details on the problems that continue to plague software development, as well as an overview of Agile software development and the origins of Lean and its unique approach to improving any kind of process.

The Problem with Software Development

Have you ever worked on a software development project that:

- Went over schedule?
- Went over budget?
- Didn't meet the needs of the customer?
- Was canceled?

If you said no, you are probably fresh out of school and are still working on your first project. If you said yes, you're not alone…not by a long shot!

The actual statistics are shocking.

The 1994 CHAOS Report from the Standish Group is *the* landmark study of IT project failure. By 1994, the Standish Group had studied over 8,000 software development projects and found that only 16% were successful. This means that 84% of the projects either failed outright or had serious problems. In 2004, after 10 years of study, the number of projects included had increased to 40,000, and the success rate had improved to 29%. Although this is a significant increase, it's still nothing to brag about.

Can you think of any other industry that has such a staggeringly low success rate?

The CHAOS Study

The Standish Group survey included large, medium, and small companies across major industry segments: banking, securities, manufacturing, retail, wholesale, health care, insurance, services, and local, state, and federal organizations (365 companies in total). Over a 10-year period, it studied over 40,000 projects. In addition, it used focus groups and personal interviews to provide a qualitative context for the survey results.

The CHAOS study classified projects into three categories:

Project Succeeded
> The project was completed on time and on budget with all the features and functions that were originally specified.

Project Challenged
> The project was completed, but went over budget, over the time estimate, and offered fewer features and functions than originally specified.

Project Failed
> The project was canceled at some point during the development cycle (the study actually called this *Project Impaired*).

Figure 1-1 shows the percent of projects in each of these categories over a 10-year period.

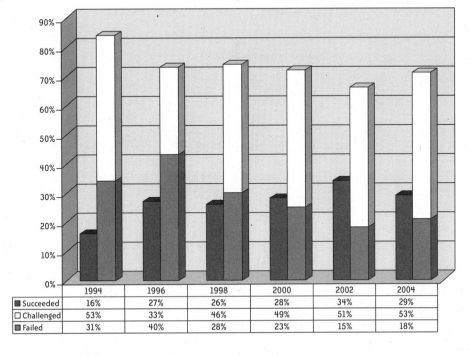

	1994	1996	1998	2000	2002	2004
■ Succeeded	16%	27%	26%	28%	34%	29%
□ Challenged	53%	33%	46%	49%	51%	53%
■ Failed	31%	40%	28%	23%	15%	18%

FIGURE 1-1. CHAOS study data

As you can see, the success rate improved over time, but at a glacial pace: 1.3% a year. At this rate, successful projects won't even break the 50% mark until the year 2020!

In fairness, some experts disagree with the definition of success used by the CHAOS study. They point out that many projects that have been classified as challenged have gone on to deliver very successful products. However, even if you take this into account, the success rate still leaves a lot of room for improvement.

The Waterfall Method

So the question is: why is the failure rate so high? A large part of the blame can be traced back to the widespread adoption of the *Waterfall* method.

The Waterfall model of software development divides development into a set of distinct phases that are performed sequentially: requirements, design, implementation, testing, deployment, and maintenance (see Figure 1-2). Development is seen as flowing steadily downward (like a waterfall) through these phases. Each phase has a beginning and an end, and once you move onto the next phase, you never go back (just as water does not flow uphill).

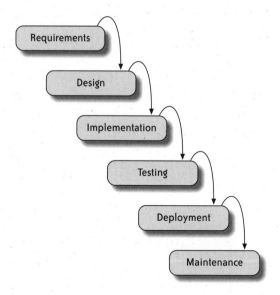

FIGURE 1-2. Waterfall model

The Waterfall method has an appealing air of simplicity. Managers like the series of fixed milestones that seem to make it easy to track a project's progress. However, this manageability is an illusion because this model does not allow for change.

Software development is a highly dynamic process and change is inevitable. During implementation you'll find problems with the design. Customers don't know precisely what they want ahead of time, and that will change the requirements.

Studies show that the Waterfall method is positively correlated with reduced productivity, increased defect rates, and project failure. Why, then, was the Waterfall method so widely promoted, and how did it become so entrenched in the face of so much evidence that it did not work?

A historical accident

Winston Royce first described the Waterfall method in a 1970 paper titled, "Managing the Development of Large Software Systems" (Technical Papers of the Western Electronic Show and Convention). This paper is often cited as if it validates the Waterfall model, but it actually does the opposite. People who use Royce's paper to support the Waterfall method must not have read this paper carefully because it explicitly says that the Waterfall method "is risky and invites failure." The paper then proceeds to advocate an iterative development style.

The Waterfall method would likely have slowly faded away, but in the 1980s it became the Department of Defense (DoD) standard for the development and procurement of software with the release of DOD-STD-2167. Eventually, the DoD realized that the Waterfall method was not working and in 1994 replaced DOD-STD-2167 with MIL-STD-498, which supports iterative development.

However, the damage was done, and a strong mindset with a bias toward Waterfall development had become ingrained. The Lightweight methods of the 1990s and the Agile methods of the early 2000s have started to turn this around, but there is a long way to go. Many people who are not familiar with the evidence are still staunch supporters of the Waterfall method.

The Agile Success Story

The Agile software development methodologies were the first attempts to improve the software development situation, with Lean coming onto the software scene much later.

Most of the Agile methodologies, like Extreme Programming (XP) and Scrum, actually predate the Agile Manifesto (which we will discuss shortly). In fact, using the term "Agile" to refer to these methods of software development was coined at the famous Snowbird meeting that created the Agile Manifesto.

In the 1990s there was a growing dissatisfaction with the prevalent heavy software development methodologies and processes. Using these processes did not solve any of the endemic problems of software development: high project failure rate, low software quality, and generally unhappy customers.

This spawned a number of alternative methodologies, including XP, Scrum, Dynamic Systems Development Method (DSDM), Crystal, and Feature Driven Development (FDD), that were collectively known as Lightweight methods. The term "Lightweight" was meant to distinguish them from the predominant heavyweight methods of the time. Their creators were not happy with the term "Lightweight" because it seemed to imply that these methods were less comprehensive or less important.

It became increasingly apparent that these Lightweight methods had a lot in common with each other. So, in February of 2001, a group of 17 of the leading independent thinkers about software development gathered at the Snowbird ski resort in Utah to try to find common ground. The roster of this two-day gathering included many of the most prominent personalities in software development at the time: Kent Beck, Mike Beedle, Arie van Bennekum, Alistair Cockburn, Ward Cunningham, Martin Fowler, James Grenning, Jim Highsmith, Andrew Hunt, Ron Jeffries, Jon Kern, Brian Marick, Robert C. Martin, Steve Mellor, Ken Schwaber, Jeff Sutherland, and Dave Thomas.

Three significant things came out of the now-famous Snowbird gathering: the decision to use the term "Agile," the Agile Manifesto, and the Agile Alliance. The Agile Alliance (*http://www .agilealliance.org/*) is a nonprofit organization that exists to further the development and dissemination of information regarding Agile processes.

As stated earlier, no one was happy with the term "Lightweight." Alistair Cockburn articulated this nicely when he said, "I don't mind the methodology being called light in weight, but I'm not sure I want to be referred to as a 'Lightweight' attending a 'Lightweight methodologists' meeting. It sounds like a bunch of skinny, feebleminded people trying to remember what day it is." And thus, we now have "Agile."

The Agile Manifesto

The Agile Manifesto (formally called the *Manifesto for Agile Software Development*) is a model of simplicity. Written by Kent Beck et al., it eloquently states the four core values that form the philosophical bedrock of all Agile methodologies:

> We are uncovering better ways of developing software by doing it and helping others do it. Through this work we have come to value:
>
> - **Individuals and interactions** over processes and tools
> - **Working software** over comprehensive documentation
> - **Customer collaboration** over contract negotiation
> - **Responding to change** over following a plan
>
> That is, while there is value in the items on the right, we value the items on the left more.

The wording of the Agile Manifesto was carefully crafted to communicate the intended message. By saying, "We are uncovering better ways of developing software," they showed that they didn't have all the answers and were still on a learning journey of discovery. Just as important was the next part, "by doing it and helping others do it," which meant that they were actively engaged in using these "better ways" (no ivory-tower theoretical advice here) and were sharing what they learned with others (not telling people what to do).

Each of the four value statements in the Agile Manifesto lists two things and states that both items are important, but the first item is higher priority. Martin Fowler and Jim Highsmith described this very succinctly in their August 2001 article in *Dr. Dobb's Journal* titled "The Agile Manifesto":

> The Alliance recognizes the importance of process and tools, with the additional recognition that the interaction of skilled individuals is of even greater importance. Similarly, comprehensive documentation is not necessarily bad, but the primary focus must remain on the final product—delivering working software. Therefore, every project team needs to determine for itself what documentation is absolutely essential.

> Contract negotiation, whether through an internal project charter or external legal contract, isn't a bad practice, just an insufficient one. Contracts and project charters may provide some boundary conditions within which the parties can work, but only through ongoing collaboration can a development team hope to understand and deliver what the client wants.

Plans *are* important, but they shouldn't be rigid, unchanging plans. The ability to respond to changes is critical to the success of most software development projects.

In addition to enumerating the four Agile values, the authors of the Agile Manifesto further refined what they meant in those value statements by listing a number of principles that they follow as a direct result of those values:

- Our highest priority is to satisfy the customer through early and continuous delivery of valuable software.
- Welcome changing requirements, even late in development. Agile processes harness change for the customer's competitive advantage.
- Deliver working software frequently, from a couple of weeks to a couple of months, with a preference to the shorter timescale.
- Business people and developers work together daily throughout the project.
- Build projects around motivated individuals. Give them the environment and support they need, and trust them to get the job done.
- The most efficient and effective method of conveying information to and within a development team is face-to-face conversation.
- Working software is the primary measure of progress.

- Agile processes promote sustainable development. The sponsors, developers, and users should be able to maintain a constant pace indefinitely.

- Continuous attention to technical excellence and good design enhances agility.

- Simplicity—the art of maximizing the amount of work not done—is essential.

- The best architectures, requirements, and designs emerge from self-organizing teams.

- At regular intervals, the team reflects on how to become more effective, then tunes and adjusts its behavior accordingly.

Agile Methodologies

There are a fair number of formal software development methodologies that fall within the Agile camp. While they vary in their specific activities and artifacts, they all use short time-boxed iterations that deliver working software at the end of each iteration (the length of the iterations varies between methodologies). Figure 1-3 shows the typical Agile process.

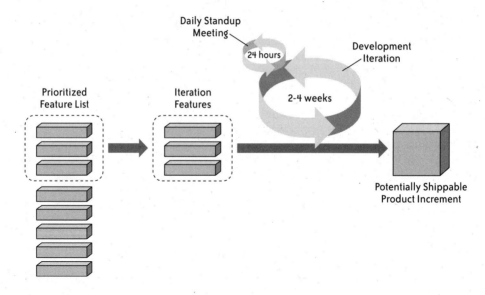

FIGURE 1-3. Typical Agile process

All Agile methodologies share a number of core practices (either formally or informally). These core practices also support Lean software development and are the subject of the second half of this book.

Some of the more commonly used Agile methodologies include:

- Scrum

- XP

- Crystal
- FDD
- Unified Process (UP)
- DSDM

These methods all began at different times in the 1990s as a response to the failure of the Waterfall method. There has been a great deal of cross-fertilization of ideas and techniques between these methods.

Scrum has successfully taken the Agile approach and stripped it down to the essentials. The result is one of the simplest and easiest-to-implement Agile methodologies that still provides the benefits of Agile software development.

XP has a rich set of interlocking practices that can feel overwhelming to those uninitiated in the Agile way, but XP gets credit for popularizing most of the core practices that have been adopted by the other methodologies. XP has probably done more to raise the awareness of Agile software development than any other methodology.

Crystal is actually a family of methodologies created by Alistair Cockburn. The actual processes and practices vary depending on a project's size and criticality or complexity.

FDD is unique among the Agile methodologies in that its perspective centers on creating domain models for the system being developed, which then organizes development around features that implement the model.

UP is generally considered to be one of the more "heavyweight" of the Agile processes, although it was intended to be tailored and not implemented in a heavy manner. Regardless, this has led to a number of variants, including the Rational Unified Process (RUP), the Agile Unified Process (AUP), and the Enterprise Unified Process (EUP).

DSDM is more formal than most of the other Agile methods, fully specifying many different roles, processes, and artifacts. A notable feature is the prioritizing of requirements according to the *MoSCoW* rules:

M
>   Must-have requirements

S
>   Should have if at all possible

C
>   Could have, but not critical

W
>   Won't have this time, but potentially later

The Lean Success Story

**It's only the last turn of a bolt that tightens it—the rest is
just movement.**

—Shigeo Shingo

It is only recently that the Lean principles have been applied to software development. In the beginning it all started with Lean manufacturing (some 40 to 60 years ago, depending on when you start the clock). Of course, it wasn't called Lean back then. It was the Toyota Production System, or Just-In-Time manufacturing. James Womack, Daniel Jones, and Daniel Roos coined the term "Lean" in their 1990 book, *The Machine That Changed the World* (Harper Perennial).

Lean is a mindset, a way of thinking about how to deliver value to the customer more quickly by finding and eliminating waste (the impediments to quality and productivity). This philosophy is expressed in a set of principles that have proven remarkably applicable to a wide range of business activities. The Lean principles have been used successfully in areas as diverse as the supply chain, the office, engineering, and (of course) software development.

First, we'll take a look at the roots of Lean thinking with a short history of how Lean developed in manufacturing. In Chapter 2, we'll show you how you can apply Lean thinking to software development and how it differs from Agile.

A Whirlwind History of Lean

To really appreciate the emergence of Lean production and its derivatives, you have to understand what it was replacing (or competing with): mass production.

Henry Ford popularized mass production (which had itself replaced craft production) with the assembly-line manufacture of the Model T in 1913. Mass production is used to produce large quantities of goods at a low unit cost. It divides the manufacturing process into small steps that can be carried out by unskilled workers, and it relies on the use of high-precision machinery and standardized, interchangeable parts.

The drawback of mass production is its inflexibility. Since a mass production assembly line is so expensive to set up (and difficult to alter), it is only economical if it is going to produce large quantities of the same thing.

In 1945, in post-war Japan, the president of Toyota Motor Company, Kiichiro Toyoda, said that the Japanese automobile industry would not survive if it did not "catch up with America in three years." This did not happen within three years (the Japanese automobile industry survived anyway), but it did lead to the creation of the Toyota Production System by Taiichi Ohno.

Taiichi Ohno realized that the American mass production system would not work in Japan. The domestic automobile market was too small and there was a significant demand for variety in automobiles, from small economical cars to larger, luxury cars—a poor fit for mass production. Out of necessity, Taiichi Ohno experimented with many ideas and techniques that eventually evolved into the Toyota Production System.

Taiichi Ohno described the Toyota Production System as "a system for the absolute elimination of waste." He wasn't kidding. By the early 1990s, Toyota was 60% more productive with 50% fewer defects than its non-Lean competitors. According to Ohno, this striking advantage rested on two pillars: Just-In-Time and autonomation.

Just-In-Time

In the 1950s, a Japanese delegation from Toyota visited American businesses to study their methods. They visited Ford Motor Company, the industry leader, but they were not impressed. They were particularly appalled by the large amounts of inventory and the unevenness of the amount of work performed in different parts of the factory.

However, when they visited an American supermarket, they were impressed with the way in which products were reordered and restocked only after customers purchased them. This *pull system* inspired Taiichi Ohno to create Just-In-Time, which strives to keep inventories at each manufacturing step as low as possible (preferably zero). It is about providing the right material, in the right amount, at the right time, and in the right place.

According to Ohno, inventory is waste that costs the company money. Even worse, inventory hides problems in the production system. This includes problems such as inadequate capacity, inflexible equipment, and unreliable equipment. A major contribution of a Just-In-Time system is that it exposes the causes of inventory-keeping so that they can be addressed.

Autonomation (Jidoka)

Autonomation is a combination of the words *autonomous* and *automation*. It describes machines that automate a process but are also intelligent enough to know when something is wrong and stop immediately. This kind of machine can run unattended (autonomously) while providing workers with full confidence that it is operating flawlessly. It doesn't have to be monitored, and it needs human attention only when it stops.

When it detects an abnormal condition, the machine will stop itself and a worker will halt the production line. This focuses everyone's attention on finding the root cause of the problem and fixing it so that it will not recur. In this way, autonomation prevents the production of defective components that would otherwise disrupt the production line or result in more costly rework at a later stage.

Waste (Muda)

The overarching goal of Lean production (or any form of Lean) is to deliver value to the customer more quickly, and the primary way to do this is to find and eliminate waste. On the surface this may seem like a simple thing, but exactly what is and what is not waste isn't always obvious. Shigeo Shingo, who codeveloped the Toyota Production System with Taiichi Ohno, identified seven kinds of waste (described in the DOTWIMP sidebar).

DOTWIMP: THE SEVEN DEADLY WASTES

Lean has some pretty strict views on waste. Shigeo Shingo identified seven types of waste that are easily remembered by using the acronym *DOTWIMP*:

Defects
> This is perhaps the most obvious type of waste. Lean focuses on preventing defects instead of the traditional "find and fix" mentality.

Overproduction
> Producing more than is needed, or producing it before it is needed. It is often visible as the storage of materials.

Transportation
> The unnecessary movement of parts between processes. When you move material and parts between factories, work cells, desks, or machines, no value is created.

Waiting
> People or parts waiting for the next production step.

Inventory
> All material, work-in-progress, and finished products that are not being processed. Inventory beyond the bare minimum consumes productive floor space and delays the identification of problems (if you've got plenty of spares, there's no incentive to fix quality-related problems).

Motion
> People or equipment moving or walking more than is needed to perform the processing.

Processing
> Overprocessing beyond the standard required by the customer. This adds additional cost without adding additional value.

Additional eighth waste: underutilization of people
> This is often cited as an additional type of waste beyond the original seven, and it refers to the underutilization of the worker's creativity and resourcefulness.

A key Lean activity is to break down a process into a map of its individual steps and identify which steps add value and which steps do not—the waste. This is known as a *value stream map*. The goal, then, is to eliminate the waste (*muda*) and improve the value-added steps (*kaizen*). The waste is further subdivided into two categories: non-value-added but necessary (given the current state of the system), and pure waste. Pure waste is easy to deal with—it can be eliminated immediately.

So, there are two key Lean skills: knowing what the customer values, and knowing how to spot waste.

LEAN SPEAK

In the world of Lean, it is very common to encounter a number of Japanese words. It may seem strange and unfamiliar at first, but you will get used to it. Here's a short primer on a few of the more common terms:

Andon
> Means "light" in Japanese. In a Lean environment, it is a visual device (usually a light or a board of lights) that gives the current status of a production system, signaling any problems (typically, green = OK, yellow = needs attention, and red = urgent/production stopped).

Jidoka
> Autonomation, the ability of a machine to inspect its work and operation and to notify a human if a problem is detected.

Kaizen
> The continuous, incremental improvement of an activity to create more value with less waste.

Kanban
> A signaling system used to signal the need for an item, typically using things like index cards, colored golf balls, or empty carts.

Muda
> Waste that consumes resources but produces no value.

Lean Principles

Taiichi Ohno started with Just-In-Time and autonomation, the two pillars of the Toyota Production System. Modern-day Lean has settled on five principles and a wide array of practices that have been distilled from the Toyota Production System and the experiences of other companies that have followed Toyota's lead. These five principles are identified as *Value, Value Stream, Flow, Pull,* and *Perfection*:

Value
> Value is defined by the customer. What does the customer value in the product? You have to understand what is and what is not value in the eye of the customer in order to map the value stream.

Value stream
> Once you know what the customer values in your product, you can create a value stream map that identifies the series of steps required to produce the product. Each step is

categorized as either value-added, non-value-added but necessary, or non-value-added waste.

Flow

The production process must be designed to flow continuously. If the value chain stops moving forward (for any reason), waste is occurring.

Pull

Let customer orders pull product (value). This pull cascades back through the value stream and ensures that nothing is made before it is needed, thus eliminating most in-process inventory.

Perfection

Strive for perfection by continually identifying and removing waste.

In the next chapter, we will see how these Lean principles can be applied to software development.

CHAPTER TWO

Applying Lean to Software Development

Everything should be made as simple as possible, but not simpler.

—Albert Einstein

Aren't Lean and Agile just two names for the same thing?

This is a common question and a common misconception. The short answer is no, they are not the same. But you want the long answer, don't you?

It's easy to see why this misconception exists. Lean and Agile share the same goals: to increase the productivity of software development while simultaneously increasing the quality of the resulting software. To compound the confusion, the practices that make up the various Agile methodologies also support the Lean principles.

Agile has a different perspective from Lean and, generally, has a narrower focus. Conversely, Lean takes a wider view, preferring to look at the entire business context in which the software development is done. Lean views Agile software development methodologies as valid supporting practices of Lean software development.

Lean Software Development

In 2003, Mary and Tom Poppendieck published the first thorough mapping of Lean principles to software development in their book, *Lean Software Development: An Agile Toolkit for Software Development Managers* (Addison-Wesley Professional), and they refined this mapping in their second book, *Implementing Lean Software Development: From Concept to Cash* (Addison-Wesley Professional, 2006).

Most subsequent writings about Lean Software Development have followed the Poppendiecks' lead and used the seven principles they identified:

- Eliminate waste
- Build quality in
- Create knowledge
- Defer commitment
- Deliver fast
- Respect people
- Optimize the whole

Let's take a closer look at each of these seven principles.

Eliminate Waste

This is a rather large category, and rightfully so, since the main thrust of Lean is the elimination of waste. Remember DOTWIMP, the seven deadly wastes? Let's see what the software development equivalents of *defects, overproduction, transportation, waiting, inventory, motion,* and *processing* would be.

Defects → defects

This one is easy. A defect is a defect, whether you're talking about manufacturing a physical product or developing software. Defects cause expensive rework, which is always non-value-added waste. The focus in a Lean environment is on preventing defects, whereas traditional development focuses on finding defects after they have already occurred. Defects are especially expensive when detected late.

In Lean, when a defect is found, the response is to find the root cause of the defect and make changes that will ensure the defect cannot recur. In software development, this means having a suite of automated tests that prevent defects from slipping into the software undetected. When a defect does slip through, a new test is created to detect that defect so that it cannot pass through undetected again.

Overproduction → extra features

Every line of code costs money. Over the lifetime of the software, the cost of *writing* the code is probably the smallest cost. The code must also be designed, documented, and maintained (changed, enhanced, debugged, etc.). This means that a cadre of current and future team members must repeatedly read and understand the code. The presence of the code must be taken into account in each future product change or enhancement.

The 80/20 rule applies in most software products: 80% of the user's real needs are provided by 20% of the product's features. This means the other 80% of a product's features are rarely (or never) used. At the XP 2002 Conference, the Standish Group reported that 45% of features were *never* used and that only 20% of features were used often or always. In fact, a 2001 paper titled "Improving Software Investments through Requirements Validation" (IEEE 26th Software Engineering Workshop) found that in 400 projects examined over a period of 15 years, less than 5% of the code was actually useful or used!

Even worse, when the Standish Group looked at only successful projects in their CHAOS study, they found that 64% of features were never or rarely used (see Figure 2-1). This is a *huge* waste that becomes an increasing drain on the project's resources over time. The time spent working on these features would be much better spent working on the real needs of the customer. If a feature does not address a clear customer need, it should not be created.

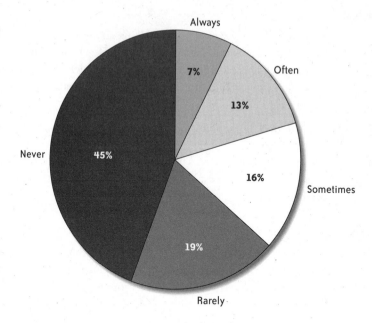

FIGURE 2-1. Percentage of delivered features actually used

Transportation → handoffs

If you have worked on large projects, this might sound familiar:

1. Analysts create a document containing all of the product's requirements and hand it off to the architects.

2. Architects take the requirements and create the product design, which they hand off to the programmers.

3. The programmers write the code to implement the design and pass the results to the QA testers.

4. The QA testers validate the resulting product against the requirements.

This is a classic Waterfall process that is replete with handoffs. A tremendous amount of knowledge is lost through each handoff simply because it is not possible to record everything that was learned, discovered, created, and known in a written form. A large amount of tacit knowledge is not passed on.

This means that the architects won't understand the requirements as deeply as the analysts, and that the programmers will not understand the design as well as the architects. This incomplete understanding will lead to errors and omissions, which will require costly rework to correct.

Even worse, the knowledge loss is compounded with each handoff. For example, if you assume that 50% of the knowledge is lost in each handoff, the programmers only receive 25% of the original knowledge, losing a whopping 75% in only two handoffs!

Try to avoid handoffs whenever possible.

Waiting → delays

Decisions are made almost constantly in every software development project. If a developer has extensive knowledge of the system being created, he will already know most of the answers to most of his questions (or be able to deduce them). However, the developer can't know everything and will invariably need to ask questions of coworkers, customers, and other stakeholders. If these people are immediately available, there is no delay and development continues at full speed.

When a question can't be immediately answered, the stage is set for all kinds of wasteful results. The developer could:

- Suspend the current task and move onto something else (which is *task switching*, a waste that is covered shortly).
- Guess the answer, which results in rework when the guess is wrong—potentially a lot of rework if it is not discovered until much later.
- Try to find the answer. Even when the developer tries to find the answer, if it's too much trouble, he'll end up guessing to save the hassle.

No matter which scenario you pick, there is waste. This is why the most productive arrangement is colocated Integrated Product Teams (IPTs) that include all team members, including the customer (or a customer representative).

Inventory → partially completed work

Simply stated, partially completed work is anything that has been started but not finished. This could be requirements (features) that haven't been coded, or code that hasn't been tested, documented, and deployed, or bugs that haven't been fixed. Rather than letting partially done work build up in queues, the Lean approach uses single-piece flow to take a feature through to deployment as rapidly as possible.

A feature is not complete until it is potentially deployable (other constraints may not allow actual deployment as often as we would like), fully documented, tested, and error-free.

Motion → task switching

Task switching and interruptions kill productivity. It takes time to get the brain focused on the task at hand so that you can understand the required factors and begin the process of problem solving. Interruptions restart this process. Task switching (a much longer interruption) causes you to have to "relearn" where you were before you can even begin to be productive again.

This is why single-piece flow is so productive. You can work completely through a feature or task without the waste of task switching.

(Over) processing → unneeded processes

Unneeded processes are pure waste. They get in the way of productivity without adding any value. They include procedures that accomplish nothing and documents that no one reads. They also include manual tasks that could be automated and procedures that make simple tasks hard.

Build Quality in

One of Taiichi Ohno's key manufacturing insights was that you cannot inspect a product for quality at the end of a production line. That approach detects problems, but it does nothing to correct them. Instead, each step in the process should be mistake-proof and self-inspecting. When a problem is detected, the entire assembly line stops until the root cause of the problem is found and corrected (so that it cannot occur again).

A famous example is the New United Motor Manufacturing, Inc. (NUMMI) automobile factory, a joint venture between Toyota and General Motors. Toyota told workers simply to do good work and to stop the line whenever something prevented them from doing their jobs. It took nearly a month to produce the first vehicle, but since each problem was solved once—permanently—the plant quickly became a leader in quality and productivity in the U.S.

Traditional software development has followed the same pattern as traditional U.S. car manufacturing: let defects slip through and get caught later by QA inspections. The Lean approach is to mistake-proof your code by writing tests as you code the features. These tests prevent subsequent changes to the code from introducing undetected defects. Chapter 4 discusses automated testing in more detail.

Create Knowledge

The point here is not to forget the lessons you have learned. Obviously, making the same mistakes over again or relearning how something works is a waste of time and effort. And it's not just you—your coworkers shouldn't have to learn something you have already figured out.

Find ways to record your team's knowledge so that you can easily locate it the next time you need it. It's hard to be specific about this because what makes sense and what will work for you is highly dependent upon the context. However, it is generally best to store a given piece of knowledge closest to its source.

For example, say you are adding a feature to a system and you have to read through the code to understand how a subsystem works. What you learn should be recorded somewhere. You could add it to a detailed design document, but it would be much more useful to record it as a comment in the code. After all, the next time someone needs to know this information, he is likely to be looking at the code—just like you.

As you architect, design, and code, you will constantly be considering alternatives and making decisions. When you do make a decision, consider recording why you chose one alternative over another. Sometimes this knowledge can be a useful timesaver in the future, but sometimes it can be overkill. Use your best judgment and try to maintain a useful balance.

Defer Commitment

The best decisions are made when you have the most information available. If you don't *have* to make a particular decision now, wait until later when you have more knowledge and information. But don't wait too long, either—lack of a decision should not hold up other aspects of the project.

Wait until the last responsible moment to make an irreversible decision.

Let's take the case where you must commit to an architectural choice. First, determine when the last responsible moment for that decision is. Use the interim time to accumulate knowledge about the real needs of the other components of the system. Use that time to explore the characteristics of alternative choices.

For example, would a simple dispatch queue work, or does the system require a publish-subscribe messaging engine? What choices lie between these two extremes? The best approach to take, if you can, is to try both alternatives and eventually choose the one that best meets the system's needs.

This is called *set-based design*. With set-based design you simultaneously pursue multiple solutions, eventually choosing the best one.

A classic example of this approach was the design of the Toyota Prius. The requirements for the Prius did not specify a hybrid engine; they only stated that the car should get exceptionally good gas mileage. Several competing engine designs were developed simultaneously. The hybrid engine was chosen at the last responsible moment (when there was just enough time to get the Prius into production by its target release date).

This might seem like waste, but in reality, making the wrong choice could have dramatically reduced the success of the Prius, resulting in wasteful lost opportunity.

Deliver Fast

Software development is an abstract endeavor. Yet most of us (including our customers) work best when dealing with concrete things. When we can see, touch, and feel something, it becomes real, and our brains can more easily think about what works and what doesn't. Our imaginations can dream of features or capabilities that we didn't realize we needed.

This is why software requirements are so volatile. The Waterfall approach would have you waiting until the end of the project to get customer feedback based on the actual use of the software, and that is why the Waterfall process is so prone to failure.

"Deliver fast" means developing features in small batches that are delivered to the customer quickly, in short iterations. These features can be implemented and delivered before the associated requirements can change. This means that the customer has an opportunity to use these features (which are now concrete) to provide feedback that can change the other requirements *before* they are implemented.

The completion of each short iteration provides an opportunity to change and reprioritize the requirements based on real feedback and use. The end result is a product that more closely meets the real needs of the customer, while simultaneously eliminating the tremendous amount of waste and rework created by the requirements churn—truly a win-win situation.

Respect People

This is a lofty altruism that is also the down-home truth. As Mary and Tom Poppendieck said in *Implementing Lean Software Development*, "Engaged, thinking people provide the most sustainable competitive advantage."

Respect for people means trusting them to know the best way to do their jobs, engaging them to expose flaws in the current process, and encouraging them to find ways to improve their jobs and the surrounding processes. Respect for people means recognizing them for their accomplishments and actively soliciting their advice.

Don't waste your most valuable resource—the minds of your team members!

Optimize the Whole

This is an important part of Lean thinking no matter where Lean is being applied, and Lean software development is no exception. Whenever you optimize a local process, you are almost always doing so at the expense of the whole value stream (this is suboptimizing).

If you don't have control over the entire value stream, you may be forced to suboptimize a piece of it. In general, though, you should always attempt to include as much of the value stream as you can when you try to optimize a process.

Lean Versus Agile

So, what is so different about Lean and Agile software development? On the surface, not too much.

Both Lean and Agile software development aim to improve the quality of the software (as perceived by the customer) as well as the productivity of the software development process. They both value (and even welcome) the changes in requirements that will almost certainly occur over the course of the project. They both place the highest value on delivering software that meets the customer's real needs (not the initial perceived customer needs).

The difference is in the underlying perspective and philosophy...the mindset.

Agile mostly concerns itself with the specific practice of developing software and the project management that surrounds that software development. Agile methods do not generally concern themselves with the surrounding business context in which the software development is taking place.

Lean principles, on the other hand, can be applied to any scope, from the specific practice of developing software to the entire enterprise where software development is just one small part. It is even common in Lean manufacturing to go outside the company and include suppliers in the scope of Lean process improvement. The larger the scope, the larger the potential benefits.

Most Lean efforts start out small and expand their scope over time, realizing more and more benefits in the process. In any case, it can be safely said that Lean views all Agile methodologies as valid supporting practices.

The primary focus of Agile software development is on close customer collaboration and the rapid delivery of working software as early as possible. Lean sees that as worthwhile, but its primarily focus is on the elimination of waste in the context of what the customer values.

A key Lean tool for detecting and eliminating waste is the *value stream map* (VSM). The VSM is a map-like diagram of all activities that take place from beginning to end—for example, from when the customer requests a new feature to when that new feature is delivered to the customer. Each step is then identified as value-added (from the customer's perspective), non-value-added, or non-value-added but necessary. VSMs are covered in more detail in Chapter 9.

Finally, Agile has a fair number of formal methodologies, whereas Lean has no formal methodologies. Lean, instead, has a toolkit of recommended practices from which to choose.

In fact, when implementing Lean software development, it is quite common to pick a lightweight Agile methodology as a starting point and begin applying other Lean tools (such as VSM) from there.

For those of you who want to take this approach, we recommend using Scrum. Scrum provides all the essentials and has a very low learning curve. Most people find it easy to learn Scrum in just a few days.

Getting Started

The journey of a thousand miles must begin with a single step.

—Chinese Proverb

If traditional and Waterfall-style software development are such failures, and if Lean and Agile software development are so much better, what is stopping everyone from switching? Of course, there are many, many reasons. This book is aimed squarely at what we think are two of the biggest reasons: fear and confusion.

Back in the days when the name IBM was almost synonymous with computers, there was a widespread saying that "no one ever got fired for buying IBM." The point was that buying a computer from IBM was safe. It didn't matter whether the project was a success or a failure; no one would blame you for going with IBM. The inverse implication was that if you went out on a limb and purchased a competitor's computer, you'd definitely get blamed if anything went wrong.

Moving to Lean or Agile software development practices can elicit the same kind of fear. Sticking with the current method of developing software can seem like a safe path, whereas pushing for Lean or Agile software development practices might feel like going out on a limb and exposing your career to unnecessary risk.

Perhaps you can imagine yourself having just convinced your boss to let your team use that hot new Agile methodology on your new project, selling him on the promise of higher productivity and higher quality. Now your neck is on the line to deliver. There are so many new practices to understand and implement, and you're not really sure how to fit them all together.

Then management unknowingly sabotages your nascent efforts by periodically "borrowing" a teammate to solve some high-priority problem on another project. Or maybe they just add new features without extending the deadline (but hey, you're doing Agile, so you can handle changes, right?).

Even worse, you don't have enough experience to recognize the serious impact that this will have on your delivery promises (and deal with it appropriately). In the end, you get blamed for the project running behind schedule and over budget. And to compound your misery, you just "proved" to management that Agile doesn't work!

This is the kind of fear that holds many people back.

Add to this the confusion created by too many choices, and you've got the perfect recipe for paralysis!

SO MANY QUESTIONS

Making changes to your development process can be a daunting task, especially if you are learning that process as you go. You may find yourself thinking along the following lines and, believe us, you're not alone:

Should I go with Agile or Lean? If I choose Agile, there are so many methodologies—which one is best for me? I don't have time to read about all of them, so how do I choose? OK, I'll just pick one, but there are so many new things to learn, and I'm supposed to tailor it to my needs. How do I know what to use and what to leave out?

If I leave out something really important, maybe I won't really be doing Agile and my project will fail. Maybe I should just play it safe and do everything. But that's more work than what I was doing before —how is that Agile? Maybe I should go for Lean.

I could do a value stream map, but this new project hasn't even started yet, and I don't know how to find waste in a development process that I haven't even decided on yet. I see that there are a bunch of recommended Lean software development practices, but which ones should I use? All of them?

This is too confusing. I've got serious mental overload here....

There are plenty of books, articles, and other published material that give you the gamut of possible practices and approaches. Agile methodologies that you don't understand can seem intimidating and complex, especially if they have to be tailored and you don't have the knowledge and experience to do so.

Lean software development provides little guidance beyond giving you a heap of possible practices. This means that you must decide what to use (or not to use) and when to use it. Once again, this is difficult if you don't have the knowledge and experience to make those decisions.

The Good News

Don't despair; there is good news. In this book, we're going to take a different approach, an approach that will let you incrementally adopt Lean and Agile practices at your own pace. As you do so, you will gain the knowledge and experience needed to make the decisions outlined in the previous section.

A number of practices are universally found in nearly all Agile methodologies and Lean software development implementations. Each practice, on its own, will give you productivity and/or quality benefits. You can adopt these practices in any order that you wish (with a couple of exceptions), but we present them here in the order that we think provides the most return for your effort:

Practice 1
> Automated Testing

Practice 2
> Continuous Integration

Practice 3
> Less Code

Practice 4
> Short Iterations

Practice 5
> Customer Participation

This book devotes a chapter to each of the practices just listed, along with a couple of prerequisite practices that you are probably already using (source code management and scripted builds, covered in the next chapter).

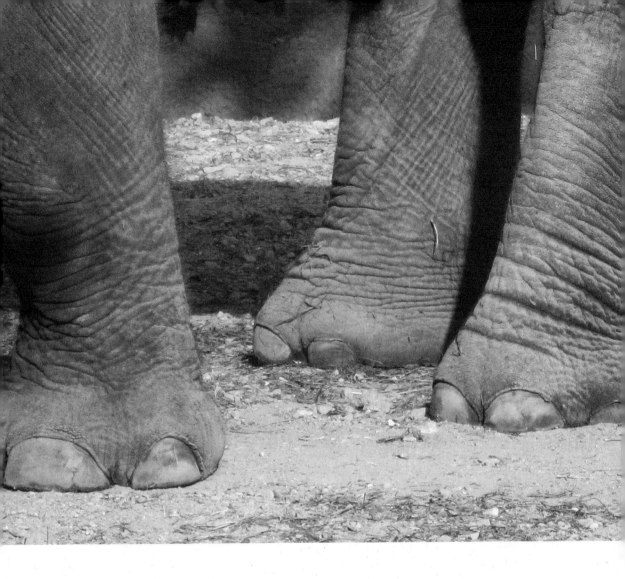

CHAPTER THREE

Practice 0: Source Code Management and Scripted Builds

Practices required for any development team larger than zero.

—Mike Sullivan

About Zero Practices

You're probably wondering, "What's the deal with these zero-level practices? Why not just start with one?" This is a book about Lean practices and, specifically, which practices give you the most bang for your buck.

However, there are some practices that you should be using whether you are trying to adopt Lean practices or not. These are not really Lean practices, but they are necessary prerequisites. That's why we refer to them as zero-level practices.

If you're not already using these practices, forget about everything else (for now), stop what you're doing, and get with the program. Seriously, these are fundamental practices that you need to be following before you try any additional improvements.

The two zero-level practices we're talking about here are *source code management* (SCM) and *scripted builds*.

Many books and articles talk about the tools you use to implement these practices but fail to address the common model of use behind them. In this chapter we give an overview of these important topics, along with a short synopsis of the functional side of each practice. In Appendix A you will find links to more in-depth material to help you implement these practices with the tool of your choice.

Source Code Management

SCM, also known as revision control or version control, basically means keeping all of your source code and other project artifacts in a central repository that maintains a complete version history of every single file.

There are both centralized and distributed flavors of version control systems. We introduce the basic concepts using a centralized system because they are more widely used. Later in the chapter we discuss the minor differences between the two flavors and why one may suit your team better than the other.

Though each SCM system has its own nomenclature, especially for the more advanced set of commands, there are several basic operations common to all systems. Whenever you want to get the current code from an existing project, you can *check out* a version of that repository. You can then *add, modify,* and *remove* files by *checking in* changes, and you can also *update*, which downloads the changes that the rest of your team has made to the repository since your checkout or last update.

Benefits

Versioning is the most basic and important capability an SCM system provides. The SCM system stores a complete revision history of every change made to every file. Each modification is assigned a revision number, and you can access prior versions in a multitude of convenient ways. If you check in a change and then discover some unintended consequences, it is easy to *revert* to the previous working version.

If you discover a bug, you can temporarily go back to a version before the bug was introduced, and then do a *diff* between that and the current version to see exactly what was changed. It's easy to diff between the current and past versions of a single file or even the entire repository!

In most SCM systems, you can also use *tags* to mark a specific version of the code. This is really useful if you want to mark a release of your software. You can roll back to a tagged version just as you can to a date or a revision number. The ability to easily access prior versions is not just a convenience; it provides a safety net that allows your team to fearlessly make changes to your software.

Your SCM system also makes it easier to effectively collaborate and communicate in a team environment. Whenever a developer checks in a change, the system stores metadata about who made the revision and when it occurred. This data is searchable and can help in a number of situations. For example, if a new member of the team is getting up to speed on a section of code, he can look through the history to find out who created the file and who has been modifying it over time. He can use this data to determine the best person to ask for a peer review or to team with for a design decision or a tricky bug.

SCM provides a shared workspace that helps the team document and share designs and ideas. Documentation is most useful when it is kept up-to-date and when it is close to the code. If your team stores documentation and design artifacts alongside the code in your repository, it is much more likely to be used and kept up-to-date. It will also have the same revision history as the code. This means that if you extract a copy of the codebase for a particular date or tag, you will get the proper versions of both the code and the corresponding documentation.

Centralized SCM

Most mainstream SCM systems such as *Concurrent Version System (CVS)*, *Subversion*, and *ClearCase* are centralized, meaning that they use a single centralized repository to store your files. Teams usually host this repository on a server that everyone has access to, and everyone is provided full permissions so that they can both check in (to contribute) and update (to pull the latest code that the rest of the team has checked into the repository). Figure 3-1 shows this type of system.

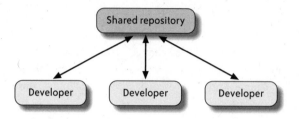

FIGURE 3-1. The centralized repository

Centralized SCM systems have been around since the early 1970s. Since SCM is a core system that the entire team relies on, these systems tend to hang around for a long time. Of the major systems still in use today, CVS is the oldest, having gained popularity in the late 1980s. ClearCase was introduced in 1990 to meet the needs of larger corporations, and Subversion is the most modern, introduced in 2000 to improve on CVS. Today, Subversion is by far the most popular choice for new projects.

In centralized systems, when you check out a copy of the repository, you download a local working copy of every file in the repository. When you make a change, the system can tell that you modified your working copy, but the copy in the central repository remains untouched. This means that you can make as many modifications as you'd like to your working copy without affecting anyone else on your team. When you are ready to share your changes with the team, you must check them in, which pushes your working copy of the files up to the centralized repository. Finally, when your team updates (downloads the latest version of the files from the repository), they will get the changes from your check-in.

As in any team environment, it is important to communicate effectively to avoid getting in each other's way. When using a centralized SCM system, there are some common idioms that most teams adopt to keep everything running smoothly:

Update before checking in changes
> Before checking in, you want to test your change against the current codebase, so always update before checking in changes. That will ensure that you aren't testing against outdated code. If your team is checking in often (as they should be), it is normal for several changes to be made to the repository in the time it takes you to make your change. The SCM system will alert you that your copy of a file is stale if you try to check in a file that someone has updated since your last update. That said, the system only looks at individual files and not at your code's dependencies. For instance, the SCM system will let you check in a *.cpp* file even if someone has modified a *.h* file that it relies on. Once you ingrain this idiom into your process, you will never be burned by testing against old code.

Don't break the build
> Since everyone on the team updates from the same codebase, developers are usually encouraged to wait until their features are tested and working before checking them in.

If you check in buggy code, no one on your team will be able to build and run the software until you fix the problem. So the quality of your code and testing directly affects your team's productivity.

Check in changes frequently

If you are going to follow the idiom of not breaking the build, you must break your implementation down into small changes to avoid working for long periods of time without the safety net of version control. Check in after each one of those small changes. If you do happen to break the build, the small scope of the change will make it easier to locate and fix the source of the problem.

Your SCM system will automatically merge for you every time you check in a change—if it can. The system can usually merge a file automatically as long as there aren't two changes in the same spot. If that happens, as it does in the following example scenario, the system kicks that responsibility back to you.

Two developers on your project each need to add a new constant to a constants file. Each checks out the file and makes his change on the last line. The first developer checks in his working copy of the file without incident. When the second developer attempts to check in, he is alerted that his working copy of the file is out-of-date and that he must update before checking in. Upon updating, the system is unable to automatically merge the repository's copy into his working copy, so he must perform the merge manually by inspecting the file and adding his content in the correct place. After he merges, he is able to check in his version of the file without incident.

On occasion, you may get stuck performing a manual merge, but in most cases it can easily be avoided with disciplined team communication and coordination.

Command line versus GUI tool

Most SCM systems offer both a command-line interface and a graphical user interface (GUI). The command-line interface provides all of the basic capabilities, but using a GUI gives you a much more intuitive interface for most operations. For example, Figure 3-2 shows which files are modified in both the command-line and visual interfaces in a folder under version control with Subversion.

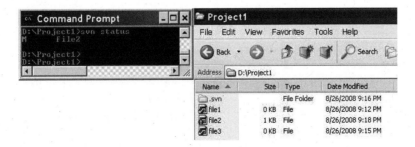

FIGURE 3-2. The command-line and TortoiseSVN visual interfaces in Subversion each show that file2 has been modified

On the left, you can see that using the command svn status provides you with the name of the modified file, denoting it with an M in the status column. On the right, you can see the familiar Windows Explorer interface and TortoiseSVN's icon overlays. The overlays are used to place checkmarks on the files that are unmodified and exclamation points on the file that has been changed. TortoiseSVN is one of the most commonly used Subversion GUI tools in the Windows environment.

Diffing, or looking at the differences (Figure 3-3), allows you to more deeply examine exactly which lines have been changed within a file.

FIGURE 3-3. A comparison of command-line and visual diffing in Subversion

As you can see on the left, the command-line interface does allow you to see which changes have been made, but even in this trivially simple example, the visual interface on the right provides a more intuitive way of looking at the differences.

Distributed SCM

Distributed SCM systems, such as git and Mercurial, are much newer than their centralized counterparts. They were created to satisfy the requirements of large open source projects, which have large codebases and distributed teams of developers. The innovative solutions they implement address some of the problems that teams of all sizes run into when using centralized SCM. That said, their relative immaturity makes it difficult to recommend their use for teams new to the concept of SCM.

The biggest difference between centralized and distributed systems is that in a distributed system you don't check out or download a working copy of the files; instead, you *clone* or download a copy of the entire functioning repository. This includes the entire revision history, and it gives you the ability to perform virtually all SCM operations locally, without connecting to a central server. In other words, a distributed system allows you to check in to your local copy of the repository (Figure 3-4).

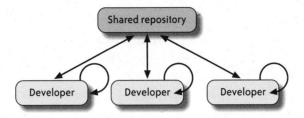

FIGURE 3-4. A centralized workflow in a distributed SCM system

In practice, changes are often not implemented and checked in one line at a time. Developers often end up making changes in several places within a file or in multiple files to implement a single change. In a centralized system, all of these subchanges go totally unversioned because the developer does not check them in until she checks the entire change into the central repository. In a distributed system, since you have a full working copy of the repository, you can check in to your local copy as often as you'd like without affecting anyone else on the team. You can check in your subchanges to version your progress within a single change. This allows you to take full advantage of the SCM safety net, even if you get stuck making a large change before checking in to the central repository. When you have completed your change, you push from your local repository up to the central repository to share it with your team.

A distributed SCM system also has other advantages and disadvantages that we will only briefly mention. You will learn more about them if you choose a distributed tool for your team's SCM. The speed of common SCM operations is extremely fast because they operate on your local copy of the repository and do not require any network access. Distributed systems can also scale to larger and more ad hoc teams by supporting workflows that do not rely on a single shared central repository. On the downside, each developer in a distributed system has his own working copy of the entire repository, so he needs to understand some advanced commands that only the SCM administrator needs to know in a centralized system.

If You Don't Know Where to Start

If you have no idea which SCM system to go with and your company doesn't have any restrictions over which software to use, we recommend using Subversion and the TortoiseSVN GUI (if you are using Windows). Subversion is far and away the most popular SCM system in use today, so it has a plethora of resources to turn to both in book and online form. It is also relatively easy to set up and get existing projects under revision control. TortoiseSVN is one of the most mature and easiest visual interfaces for Windows. Subversion also has excellent support on Linux platforms, with both a command-line interface and several popular visual tools available, such as RapidSVN.

Scripted Builds

The goal of scripted builds is to automate the entire process of building your system. As a result, your system is built the same way every time. This eliminates hidden errors and makes it easier to bring new developers into your team. It also makes it easier to test and release your software.

Many tools are available for creating scripted builds. Most development environments include a build tool, which is what teams generally use. For example, C and C++ projects normally use *make*, whereas Java projects normally use Ant. No matter which system your team uses, the goal is to have a single command or script that you can run to build all of your software. That build script should be under SCM so that you can check out your project on any machine and successfully build your system.

The most common problem that teams run into when creating a scripted build system is leaving out key components. Your build script should set all necessary environment variables, and you should include all data files and correct versions of all dependent libraries in your SCM system. It may seem like overkill to include dependent libraries, but it will make your builds more robust by guaranteeing that you are linking against tested versions of libraries instead of relying on older or newer libraries that may be installed on a target system.

You must also be vigilant in maintaining your scripted build system. It is easy to allow manual procedures to creep back into your build process, so test regularly by building on a clean system or virtual machine before it becomes a problem.

Discipline in an Integrated Environment

Using a shared codebase under SCM and a scripted build system creates an integrated environment and promotes an increased level of team interaction. If your team is disciplined about sharing and coordinating, you can maximize the benefit of your new tools.

Share

Commit as often as possible, preferably after each chunk of progress is complete. If everyone builds against your latest code, your team will discover integration problems such as bugs and design flaws very quickly, before they become more time-consuming and expensive to fix. Committing often can also improve your team morale. When each member of the team regularly updates, it makes progress more tangible and increases the sense of a shared goal, which will boost the whole team's productivity.

Coordinate

Avoid stepping on each other's toes by coordinating development and design tasks. Don't feel like you have to put this coordination off until your team meetings. You should pull together the necessary team members and address design issues as soon as they present themselves. This will both eliminate unnecessary rework and help you design code that is easy to integrate.

Summary

Once you have checked all necessary resources into a source code management system, created a fully scripted build system, and worked on your team's discipline, you are well prepared to begin your Lean journey. In the next five chapters, you will build on top of these basic practices while increasing both quality and productivity.

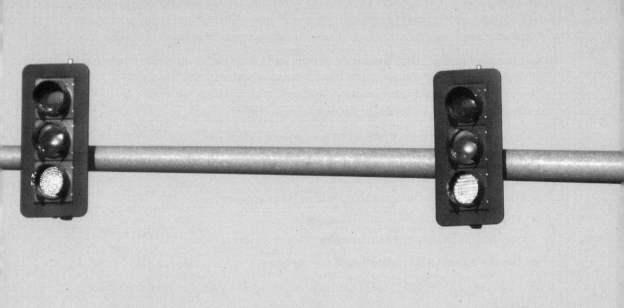

CHAPTER FOUR

Practice 1: Automated Testing

Never do manually anything that can be automated.

—Curt Hibbs

Mistake-proofing is a fundamental Lean concept. It is a central part of producing a quality product and reducing waste (by eliminating rework). This is just as true in software development as it is in manufacturing. Automated testing is the primary means of mistake-proofing in software development.

Not coincidentally, automated testing is also a cornerstone of the Agile methodologies. Automated testing is so ubiquitous in the Agile world that it is just assumed that no one would even consider writing new code without automated tests. Although this is not quite as true with legacy code, even there the trend is toward increasing use of automated testing.

Automated testing is a pretty broad term. We are using it here as an umbrella term to refer to all kinds of testing: unit testing, integration testing, acceptance testing, executable specifications testing, performance testing, load testing, story testing, test-driven development, test-first development, behavior-driven development, etc.

Each of these different types of testing have a particular focus, but they all have the following in common:

- The tests are created manually by developers
- They can all be run automatically, without human intervention
- They are run by some type of test harness
- Test failures are detected automatically
- The developer is notified when such failures occur

Automated testing supports three of the Lean software development principles described in Chapter 2:

- Eliminate waste
- Build quality in
- Create knowledge

Automated testing helps eliminate the waste of rework that occurs when defects slip through to later phases of the software development lifecycle. Such escaped defects are particularly expensive (in time, money, and reputation) when they make it all the way to deployment.

Automated testing is a primary method for building in quality. A codebase with a full suite of automated tests is self-checking and self-validating. This helps reduce the likelihood that undetected errors will be introduced into the software.

Finally, automated tests serve as living documentation on how to actually use the APIs of the codebase. This creates firsthand knowledge that developers actually trust because it is guaranteed to be accurate every time the test suite successfully executes.

Why Test?

There are numerous benefits to automated testing, and we cover them throughout this chapter, but let's start with the basics: productivity and quality. The quickest way to simultaneously increase your productivity and the quality of your software is by having a full suite of automated tests. This has been borne out through personal experience and independent studies, including a paper that Hakan Erdogmus presented at the Proceedings of the IEEE Transactions on Software Engineering (2005) titled, "On the Effectiveness of the Test-First Approach to Programming."

When a project lacks a suite of automated tests, developers are very cautious about making changes or additions, especially if they are not very familiar with the code. This means that a lot of time is spent studying code that is going to be changed, and studying the use of that code throughout the entire codebase. Even then, developers may still feel like they've missed something important. This adds a lot of time to both the development of new features and the fixing of problems.

When your project has a suite of automated tests, it acts like a safety net for the developers. Rather than spending an inordinate amount of time studying and understanding the target code, the developer can simply implement the feature (or fix the problem) with a simpler understanding of just the immediate target code. She can safely do so because she knows that any unforeseen adverse consequences will be caught by the automated tests.

When you can confidently add to or modify the code without an excessive amount of research, you can save a substantial amount of time. In addition, since problems are immediately detected and corrected, you can eliminate expensive rework that would otherwise occur if the problems were detected at a much later phase in the project.

Finally, when a developer wants to know how a piece of code works, she will usually avoid any detailed documentation because experience has shown that such documentation is usually out-of-date and, therefore, wrong. This is why developers prefer to study the code itself. Tests effectively document how pieces of code should be used, and they can be proved to be correct and up-to-date simply by running them. Because of this, developers come to rely on tests as reliable, working documentation.

CURT'S TESTING STORY

Curt well remembers his personal testing epiphany. He was working on a 20,000-line Java codebase that he had personally written, so he was intimately familiar with the code and its design. It was the first time he had decided to create a complete unit test suite as the code was being developed (now known as test-driven development, or TDD).

One day he made one of those simple changes, just three lines of localized code that couldn't possibly affect anything else in the program. What could be easier? Make the change, check out the user interface, and release the update to production. The user interface appeared to work just fine, but the change caused four unit tests to fail. These failures were in code that "could not possibly have been affected by the change"—an obviously incorrect assumption.

Had this change been deployed into production, the bug would have manifested itself in subtly corrupted data that would have been very difficult to track down (and in the meantime there would have been many irate customers). Luckily, the unit test suite caught this problem immediately after these three lines of code were written. The unit tests found the source of the problem, as well as the exact places where the resulting problems surfaced. Sorting out this problem and providing the correct fix was now fairly easy—and there were no irate customers, either!

Since that time, Curt has never written any code without tests (except for some legacy code that he did not control). Writing code without tests now seems as unthinkable as driving a car without a seat belt.

A typical excuse for not creating automated tests is that the deadlines are too tight and "we cannot spend extra time writing tests." This is a myth and a classic example of shortsighted thinking. Yes, it does take time to write these tests, but this time is more than offset by the savings of eliminating rework, reducing the cost of debugging, and reducing the fear of changing the code. Automated tests actually help you meet your deadlines!

An unexpected benefit of automated testing is that it actually improves the design of the code being tested. There are two primary reasons for this. First, when you write tests against your API, any deficiencies in the design of that API become painfully obvious because you have just become a user of that API. If you are using test-first development, you write the tests even before writing the code. Since you are using your API before it is even implemented, it is very easy to simply change the API or design to address the deficiencies. If the tests are being written after the code, minor deficiencies are usually overlooked, but major deficiencies will still trigger a redesign.

Second, when you are creating automated tests as a part of your development process, you quickly learn to design the code in a manner that ensures that it is testable. Testable code encourages the same good attributes that design and architecture experts have been preaching for years: loose coupling, minimized dependencies, and encapsulation.

A recent trend in automated testing is to write requirements in the form of executable specification tests. New testing frameworks (RSpec, JBehave, NSpec, Spector, etc.) let you write tests that describe the desired system behavior in a manner that is readable by business stakeholders and by developers. The ability to execute these tests eliminates the disconnect between requirements and code. It also means that the verification of the code against the requirements is now trivial and completely automatic. The bottom line is another big jump in both productivity and first-time quality.

In summary, having a full set of automated tests is one of the most important things you can do, because tests:

- Are bug-repellent
- Help localize defects
- Facilitate changes (act as a safety net)
- Simplify integration
- Improve code design (which also facilitates changes)
- Document the actual behavior of the code

What Is Automated Testing?

First, let's be absolutely clear about what automated testing is not: it is not running tests that are automatically created or generated by software that scans and analyzes your source code. We would call this *automatic* testing. While automatic testing may have its place (we have not yet been convinced that it offers any value), it is not the kind of testing we are talking about here. In automated testing, we are interested in checking the code's correct behavior, something that a code analysis tool cannot do.

Automated testing provides you with the ability to execute a suite of tests at the push of a button (or via a single command). These tests are crafted manually, usually by the same developers who created the code being tested. Often the boilerplate code that represents the skeleton of a test (or set of tests) will be automatically generated, but never the actual test code itself.

The Test Harness and Test Suites

A *test suite* is a collection of related tests. The tests in a suite are executed, one at a time, by a piece of software known as a *test harness*. There are many freely available, open source test harnesses. The most widely used test harness is probably the xUnit series (JUnit, NUnit, cppUnit, httpUnit, etc.). A given test harness is usually specific to a particular programming language or environment.

As the test harness cycles through the tests it is running, it will typically do a number of other things as well. Before it runs each individual test, the test harness will call the test suite's setup routine to initialize the environment in which the test will be run. Next, it runs the test, and the test harness stores information about the success or failure of the test (the test harness may also collect more information from the test describing the specifics of any failure). Finally, the test harness will call the suite's teardown routine to clean up after the test.

The test harness will then report the results of all the tests back to the initiator of the test run. Sometimes this is simply a console log, but often the test harness is invoked by a GUI application that will display the results graphically.

In the GUI case, while the tests are running, you will usually see a green progress bar that grows toward 100% as each test is completed. This progress bar will stay green as long as all the tests are succeeding. However, as soon as a single test fails, the progress bar turns red and stays red as the remaining tests are run. Other parts of the display will tell the developer the details of the failures (how many, the names of the failed tests, etc.). When a GUI test runner is integrated with an IDE, failures are usually displayed as clickable links that will open the editor to the code line where the failure occurred.

Only very small codebases would have a single suite of tests. Typically, tests are organized into a collection of test suites where each suite contains a set of related tests. For example, for unit tests in an object-oriented language, you will usually create a separate test suite for every class (or group of closely related classes). Each test in a suite for a particular class would test a single method of that class.

Using behavior-driven development (BDD) as another example, each test suite would test a single feature of the application or system, with each individual test checking a single behavior of that feature.

Running Automated Tests

You can normally run automated tests in two different ways. First, developers can manually run a subset of the tests while coding. Second, the scripted build can run the full complement of tests automatically.

As developers write code, they will periodically run the subset of tests that check the part of the application in which they are working. This helps them ensure that they haven't unexpectedly broken something. If a test fails, it is usually very easy to find the cause, since only a small amount of code has been changed since the same test ran successfully. Also, just before the developers check their changes into the source control repository, they usually run the full set of tests to make sure they haven't broken something in other parts of the system.

If test-first development (TFD) is being used, the test for new or changed code is written *before* the implementing code. This means that, initially, the test will fail (because the change hasn't yet been implemented), and the goal is to refine the application's code until the test succeeds. There is more on TFD later in this chapter.

In any case, the script that builds the application will normally run the full set of tests automatically. This helps ensure that the application or system as a whole is relatively bug-free at all times.

When continuous integration is used (Chapter 5), the application is built on a regular basis—usually at least once a day, and often many times a day. For very large applications or systems, it can take a very long time to run the full set of automated tests. In this case, it is common to select a subset of tests to run as part of the daily or intraday builds, and to only run the full set of tests nightly or weekly.

Kinds of Tests

There are many different kinds of tests. In this section we present the common categories of tests. Keep in mind that the dividing line between these categories is not always sharp, and there can be overlap and gray areas.

Unit Tests

Unit tests are the most basic type of automated test. Unit tests are usually organized with an one-to-one correspondence to the physical organization of the code being tested. This is an easy-to-understand organization, so it's not surprising that this is the most popular kind of automated testing. If you have never done any kind of automated testing, you should start with unit testing. Experienced testers, however, are starting to move to behavior testing instead of unit testing. So, if you are an adventurous novice tester, you might consider starting directly with behavior testing.

In an object-oriented language such as Java, C++, or C#, the units of code that are tested are the public methods within a class. Just as a class collects a group of related methods, a test suite for a given class will contain the unit tests for the methods within that class. There will usually be one test suite for every class.

Sometimes, when you have a small set of classes that work together intimately, you might instead have a single test suite for the group of classes. For example, if you had some kind of specialized collection class and a separate class for iterating over an instance of the collection, you would probably test both classes in a single test suite.

In functional languages such as C, Lisp, or Haskell, the units of code that are tested are the individual functions. The test suites would usually organize tests according to the natural organizational units of the target language (such as files or modules).

Examples 4-1, 4-2, and 4-3[*] show samples of unit tests in Java, C#, and C++, respectively.

EXAMPLE 4-1. Java tests using JUnit

```
//CalculatorTest.java
package test;
import static org.junit.Assert.*;
import org.junit.Test;

public class CalculatorTest {

    private Calculator calc = new Calculator();

    @Test
    public void testAdd() {
```

---

[*] Most of the code examples in this chapter have been excerpted (with permission) from the documentation of each test framework.

```
            assertSame(15, calc.add(10, 5));
    }
    @Test
    public void testSubtract() {
            assertSame(5, calc.subtract(10, 5));
    }
    @Test
    public void testMultiply() {
            assertSame(50, calc.multiply(10, 5));
    }
    @Test
    public void testDivide() {
    assertSame(2, calc.divide(10, 5));
    }
}
```

EXAMPLE 4-2. C# tests using NUnit

```
namespace account
{
  using NUnit.Framework;

  [TestFixture]
  public class AccountTest
  {
    [Test]
    public void TransferFunds()
    {
      Account source = new Account();
      source.Deposit(200.00F);
      Account destination = new Account();
      destination.Deposit(150.00F);

      source.TransferFunds(destination, 100.00F);
      Assert.AreEqual(250.00F, destination.Balance);
      Assert.AreEqual(100.00F, source.Balance);

    }
  }
}
```

EXAMPLE 4-3. C++ tests using cppUnit

```
void
MoneyTest::testConstructor()
{
  // Set up
  const std::string currencyFF( "FF" );
  const double longNumber = 1234.5678;

  // Process
  Money money( longNumber, currencyFF );

  // Check
  CPPUNIT_ASSERT_EQUAL( longNumber, money.getAmount() );
```

```
  CPPUNIT_ASSERT_EQUAL( currencyFF, money.getCurrency() );
}

void
MoneyTest::testEqual()
{
  // Set up
  const Money money123FF( 123, "FF" );
  const Money money123USD( 123, "USD" );
  const Money money12FF( 12, "FF" );
  const Money money12USD( 12, "USD" );

  // Process & Check
  CPPUNIT_ASSERT( money123FF == money123FF );
  CPPUNIT_ASSERT( money12FF != money123FF );
  CPPUNIT_ASSERT( money123USD != money123FF );
  CPPUNIT_ASSERT( money12USD != money123FF );
}

void
MoneyTest::testAdd()
{
  // Set up
  const Money money12FF( 12, "FF" );
  const Money expectedMoney( 135, "FF" );

  // Process
  Money money( 123, "FF" );
  money += money12FF;

  // Check
  CPPUNIT_ASSERT( expectedMoney == money );
  CPPUNIT_ASSERT( &money == &(money += money12FF) );
}
```

Mocks and Stubs

Ideally, a unit test should test a single unit of code in isolation, not invoking any other code unit. In practice, this is one of the biggest challenges of automated testing. Code A calls code B, which, in turn, calls code C. So, how do you test only code A?

The primary techniques used are *mocks* and *stubs*. A stub is a piece of code that does nothing but substitute for another piece of code that you don't want called. So, if code A calls code B, you can test code A in isolation by substituting a stub for code B. The stub will usually return a hardcoded value that is suitable for testing code A.

This implies that there is a way to perform this stub substitution at runtime (or at least at link time). Writing code in a way that makes this possible is what we mean when we say that you should create code that is testable. One technique is proving to be very versatile and is growing in popularity: Dependency Injection (DI), also known as Inversion of Control. DI is useful for much more than automated testing, but here we will restrict ourselves to the testing aspects.

In a traditionally written piece of code, say code A, other pieces of code that it calls (its dependencies) will be hardcoded. In other words, code A directly calls code B, code C, etc. With DI, these calls are not hardcoded. Instead, they are called through a variable or some other lookup mechanism, allowing you to switch the actual destination of the call at runtime—in our case, to a stub.

A mock is really just a more complicated set of stubs. A stub is really dumb, typically just containing a hardcoded return value. A mock is designed to substitute for a larger subsystem. As such, it pretends to be an instance of a subsystem, returning a coordinated set of values to emulate the subsystem it is replacing. A mock will usually consist of multiple stub-like functions that contain some minimal logic.

For example, you might have a mock that is designed to stand in place of a database. This mock database might read and return a set of canned responses from a text file.

There are also prewritten mocks ready to use. For example, the Java-based Spring framework includes several prewritten mocks, including one that stands in for the Java Naming and Directory Interface (JNDI) service.

Integration Tests

Where unit tests are designed to test individual units of code (in as much isolation as possible), integration tests allow you to determine how these code units work together. Sometimes this just means removing the mocks and stubs and letting the code call its real dependencies. It might also mean writing new tests that are specifically designed to test the interfaces between classes or modules. Figure 4-1 illustrates the basic differences between integration and unit testing.

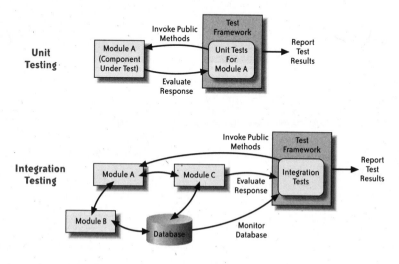

FIGURE 4-1. Unit and integration testing

Behavior Tests

Behavior testing is a recent development on the testing scene. Still, most of the leading advocates of automated testing are moving to behavior testing, lending it a great deal of advance credibility. Behavior testing is both a different perspective on testing and a new set of test harness tools to directly express this new perspective.

Behavior testing doesn't take into account the physical organization of the code or things such as classes and modules. Instead, behavior testing focuses on the individual features of the application or system and the behaviors that the application must exhibit to implement the feature. It is these behaviors that are tested.

This is best illustrated by Examples 4-4 and 4-5, which contain sample behavior tests for Ruby and Java, respectively.

EXAMPLE 4-4. Ruby behavior tests using RSpec

```
Story: transfer from savings to checking account
  As a savings account holder
  I want to transfer money from my savings account
  to my checking account
  So that I can get cash easily from an ATM

  Scenario: savings account has sufficient funds
    Given my savings account balance is $100
    And my checking account balance is $10
    When I transfer $20 from savings to checking
    Then my savings account balance should be $80
    And my checking account balance should be $30

  Scenario: savings account has insufficient funds
    Given my savings account balance is $50
    And my checking account balance is $10
    When I transfer $60 from savings to checking
    Then my savings account balance should be $50
    And my checking account balance should be $10
```

EXAMPLE 4-5. Java behavior tests using JBehave

```java
/** set balance = 50 */
public class AccountIsInCredit extends GivenUsingMiniMock {
    public void setUp(World world) {
        Mock account = (Mock) world.get("account",
                    mock(Account.class));

        account.stubs("getBalance")
               .withNoArguments()
               .will(returnValue(50));
    }
}

. . .
```

```
public class HappyScenario extends MultiStepScenario {
    public void specifySteps() {
        given(new AccountIsInCredit());
        when(new UserRequestsCash());
        then(new ATMShouldDispenseCash());
        then(new ATMShouldReturnBankCardToCustomer());
        then(new AccountBalanceShouldBeReduced());
    }
}

public class OverdrawnWithoutPermission extends MultiStepScenario {

    public void specifySteps() {
        given(new HappyScenarioWithOverdraft());
        given(new AccountHasNegativeBalanceWithoutPermission());
        when(new UserRequestsCash());
        then(new ATMShouldRefuseCash());
        then(new ATMShouldReturnBankCardToCustomer());
    }
}
```

Notice that the Ruby example reads like normal English. The Ruby programming language excels at creating domain-specific languages (DSLs) such as what you see in Example 4-4. Rest assured that this is really executable Ruby code.

Testing behaviors is closely related to the subject of the next section: executable specifications.

Executable Specifications

Another recent trend in automated tests has been the use of executable tests as specifications or requirements. These executable specifications often double as acceptance tests—when the project is completed, all of these tests should pass.

The idea of executable requirements has been developed from two separate camps. The first is Framework for Integrated Test (FIT), which uses tables on wiki pages to specify tests that are to be run by the FIT test harness. The second is a natural extension of behavior testing to a higher level of behavior that expresses the requirements of the system.

Both of these approaches to executable specifications share the same attributes: they are readable and understandable to both the business stakeholders and the software developers, and they are executable as tests by the computer.

Nonfunctional Testing

There are a number of areas in which an application or system must be tested that are not related to its functions. Here are a few of them:

- Performance testing
- Load testing

- Security (vulnerability) testing
- Compatibility testing
- Usability testing

These types of testing are much more difficult to automate than the types of testing we have presented so far. In fact, it may be impossible to satisfactorily automate some of them (how would you automate usability testing?).

Because of this, these types of testing have remained largely manual. Tools are available to assist with performance and load testing, but it is rare for them to be fully automated.

User Interface Testing

Testing a user interface, whether it is a desktop UI or the browser interface in a web application, is another testing area that has been difficult to automate. Tools are available to help automate the testing of a user interface, but they tend to be specific to a particular environment and are difficult to create and maintain.

One potential bright spot is browser-based web applications. Since the environment and technologies that underlie web applications are based on standards, it should be possible to build fairly generic tools to automate testing of the user interface. One such tool, Selenium, is written in JavaScript and runs in the browser. Selenium lets you write automated tests that can simulate the actions of a user and check for the correct responses from the application. Over time you can expect to see more tools like this.

Since it is difficult to automate user interface testing, a traditional alternative strategy is to divide the user interface code into two parts. The bulk of the code implements the "business logic" of the user interface, with a thin GUI rendering layer on top. Automated tests are then directed at the business layer.

That traditional workaround has been rendered largely obsolete by the increasing use of the Model-View-Controller (MVC) architecture. The MVC architecture produces the same separation of business logic and GUI rendering by its very nature. In an MVC architecture, the automated tests are written to test the model and controller parts.

Approaches to Testing

No matter which approach you take to testing, the most important thing is to *actually have* a set of automated tests and to strive for a level of coverage that gives you benefits that will far outweigh the costs.

It is unrealistic, and probably not worth the cost, to achieve 100% test coverage of your source code. For new code and projects that are new to automated testing, 60 to 80% code coverage for your tests is a reasonable target, although seasoned testers will strive for 80 to 95%

coverage. There are tools that will examine your source code and tests, and then tell you what your test coverage is (for example, Emma and Cobertura for Java, and NCover for .NET).

Legacy code is a different story. We have more to say about legacy code later in this chapter. For now, suffice it to say that legacy code will almost certainly start with 0% test coverage. The strategy with legacy code is to get a test harness in place, and then incrementally add tests over time—creating tests for any code that you change or enhance. This low-overhead approach will increase coverage over time and will also increase the quality and malleability of the legacy codebase.

Using Setup and Teardown

The cardinal rule of automated testing is that each individual test must be independent of any other test. Stated another way, no test can depend on the results of a previous test. If you adhere to these rules, tests can be run in any order, and any individual test can be run by itself.

Every test suite has its own setup and teardown function. The setup function's job is to initialize the test environment for the suite's tests. This includes preparing any data (data files, in-memory data, database tables, etc.) so that it is in a known, pristine state. The setup function also initializes any required libraries, subsystems, or services (for unit tests, this can be kept to a minimum by using mocks and stubs).

It is important to know that the test suite's setup is called multiple times, once before each test in the suite. This ensures a pristine test environment at the start of each test. Correspondingly, the teardown function is called after each test in the suite to clean up and release any resources allocated or initialized by setup.

Testing with Databases

Unit testing a database-driven application is often a sticking point for novice testers, and the standard canned advice is not very helpful. The traditional answer is to create a mock for your database that lets you run your tests without a database. This only works for very simple schemas and very simple tests.

In the vast majority of cases, the database schema and application are too complicated to create a mock at a reasonable cost. This means that an alternative approach must be used. Keep in mind, however, that no matter what approach is taken, the data environment must be initialized to a known state before *each test*.

A common architectural approach is to design the application with a *data abstraction layer* (DAL) that isolates the application from the fact that a database is being used. The application calls the DAL for the logical data it wants, and the DAL queries the database to get the data. This makes it easy to create alternative DALs that go elsewhere for the data (like local files) or return a canned response (in the case of a mock).

If a DAL is not feasible, you might have to use a real database in your testing. This means that you need a test database and a test set of data that you can load into the database before each test. Of course, you'll want to do this as efficiently as possible so that your tests run quickly. If your database supports nested transactions, you can load the test data into the database once, start a new transaction before each test, and then do a rollback after each test finishes.

There are tools that can help you test with a database (for example, the open source tool DbUnit).

Test-Driven Development

In TDD, you create the tests for each feature of an application before you develop the feature itself. Initially, the tests will fail because the code implementing the feature has not yet been written. You then proceed to implement the feature. You will know when you are done because the failing tests will pass.

Technically, you should always write the test first, before implementing the code. However, many projects are lenient on this rule, and the tests are often written after the feature has been implemented. This is particularly true when the implementation was the result of some exploratory programming.

Purists who want to make absolutely clear that they *always* write their tests first may say that they practice test-first development (TFD). That said, there are also some benefits to writing tests first that can make it worth striving for.

By writing tests first, you actually view the feature's API through the eyes of the user of that API. More importantly, you do so before that API has been physically created. This means that you will discover problems with the usability of the API while it is easiest to change. The result is usually a significantly better internal design.

Red, Green, Refactor

The phrase "Red, Green, Refactor" is heard often in Agile and Lean development circles. It summarizes the endless repetition of the iterative work cycle of TDD until the project is finished:

Red
> This refers to the state where you have written the test for a new feature, but you haven't yet written the implementing code. When you run the tests, they will fail, and a GUI test runner would show a "red" status.

Green
> You've written just enough code to get the tests to pass. At this point, a GUI test runner would show a "green" status.

Refactor

You designed the code to get the feature working as quickly as possible, but it may not be the best code. In this step you refactor the code to improve its structure.

Refactoring is an essential step for maintaining a high-quality codebase. To refactor means to change the code's internal structure and implementation without changing its external behavior. You can find entire books on the subject of refactoring. See Appendix A for a list of recommended resources.

Legacy Code

The traditional wisdom is that a legacy codebase slowly deteriorates over time. Changes and feature additions become increasingly costly and time-consuming to implement (you touch one thing, and 10 other things break!). Eventually, the codebase becomes so fragile that no one wants to touch it, so you consider only changes that are absolutely essential. The next time the code requires a major change, you tell management that it would be cheaper to throw it away and start over again from scratch.

It doesn't have to be that way. Instead of slowly rotting away, a legacy codebase can instead be steadily and incrementally improved so that it gets better over time. Better means easier, safer, and less costly to change. The vehicle of this miracle is (drumroll, please...) automated tests!

Michael Feathers wrote the book (literally) on how to get a legacy codebase under test. His book, *Working Effectively with Legacy Code* (Prentice Hall, 2004), is a must-read for anyone who works with legacy code (at one time or another, this applies to all of us). Feathers has a very simple definition of legacy code: "Legacy code is any code for which automated tests do not exist."

He goes to great lengths to justify this definition. If we accept it, then many of the developers reading this book probably wrote some legacy code just yesterday!

It is not easy to retrofit tests onto a legacy codebase. First, you can't just stop all other work and undertake a massive effort to add tests across an entire codebase. (Even if you could convince management to fund it, this kind of boring drudge work would be doomed to failure.) However, you can take an incremental approach where you add tests to any area of the code that you change. Even so, you will likely encounter many other problems trying to test code that was not designed to be testable.

This is where Feathers's book becomes essential reading. It is basically an encyclopedia of the problems you will run into while retrofitting tests onto legacy code, and it includes a series of techniques for dealing with each type of problem.

Behavior-Driven Development

BDD is at the current cutting edge of the automated testing field. As such, fewer tools, frameworks, and other resources are available. At the same time, BDD promises some of the greatest benefits of any automated testing technique. Even if you can't currently practice BDD, it is a field worth keeping up with.

BDD takes the behavior testing that we presented earlier and makes it the driving force behind design and implementation. In BDD, you write the requirements for a feature as one or more behavior tests, before any detailed design or implementation.

Since behavior tests are readable by the business stakeholders, they can be considered to be the official product requirements. The business stakeholders can sign off on them (and approve subsequent changes). Because computers can run them, they become executable specifications. Finally, once the system has been implemented, they also become executable acceptance tests.

Summary

We believe that automated testing is the most important and beneficial practice that you can adopt. When you use automated testing conscientiously, the increase in your productivity and the quality of the resulting software cannot be matched by any other single practice.

CHAPTER FIVE

Practice 2: Continuous Integration

Integration isn't easy. It can be painful, aggravating, and even depressing. It's the hill you have to climb at the end of the race to reach the finish line. Why would you want to do it continuously? Isn't one thrashing enough?

—Steve Jewett

Integration is where the whole development effort comes together. Individual components, databases, user interfaces, and system resources are all tied together and tested via the underlying architecture. Integration involves verifying that components communicate properly via public interfaces, ensuring that data formats and message contents are compatible and complete, and making sure that timing and resource constraints are obeyed. Traditional development processes treat integration as a separate phase occurring after all the pieces have been implemented, and it is typically a laborious, time-consuming process involving a lot of debugging and rework. Continuous integration, or CI, turns the traditional integration phase into an ongoing activity that occurs during the implementation of the system.

CI is not simply an integration phase spread out over the entire development cycle—at least, not the traditional integration phase you're probably used to. Continuous integration is the process of integrating small changes on a continual basis in order to eliminate a separate integration phase prior to product release. By integrating small changes at short intervals, developers can grow the product a little bit at a time while ensuring that each new piece works with the rest of the system.

Essentially, CI is a practice wherein developers integrate small changes by checking in updates to a source code management (SCM) system and building the system to ensure that nothing has been broken. A CI implementation can be as simple as building and testing all the source code or as complex as creating a fully tested, inspected, and deployable release.

CI is closely associated with the idea of completely automated builds, which create deployable products from source code in an SCM repository. CI extends the idea by performing an automated build (including testing and reporting of results) each time the codebase changes. What separates CI from automated builds is how the process is initiated. Automated builds are typically started on command by a developer or at a specific time of day; in a CI implementation, the build process starts automatically anytime a developer checks in changes to the SCM repository.

Continuous integration has several prerequisites:

Source code management
> We covered SCM in Practice 0, so you should backtrack to Chapter 3 if you don't already have it in place.

Unit testing framework
> Automated unit testing is an integral part of any useful CI implementation, so a unit testing framework and a robust set of unit tests is necessary to fully implement CI. Unit testing was covered in Practice 1, so backtrack to Chapter 4 to see how unit testing is implemented.

An end-to-end automated build
> An end-to-end automated build uses a script to control the building of the product from source code to releasable software.

A dedicated build server

You can perform CI without a machine dedicated to building software, but it is most effective with a dedicated build server. A dedicated build server helps eliminate problems arising from configuration changes caused by other activities.

Continuous integration software

Continuous integration software must do three things: detect changes in the SCM repository, invoke the scripts that build the product, and report the results of the build. The development team can write custom CI software, but it is more common to use a third-party application.

In the following sections, we'll look at the prerequisites for implementing CI and then discuss how to approach an initial implementation.

End-to-End Automated Builds

An end-to-end automated build creates a complete software product from the raw source code by invoking all required actions automatically and without intervention on the part of a developer. Implemented via build scripts (see Chapter 3), end-to-end automated builds used within a CI process (called CI builds) are characterized by three features:

- CI builds start from scratch
- CI builds are end-to-end processes
- CI builds report results automatically

Building from Scratch

CI builds start by retrieving a fresh copy of the latest source code from the SCM repository. Scripted builds used for other purposes may build only those modules that have changed, but CI builds always start from scratch. Rebuilding everything eliminates the possibility of dependency changes sneaking in undetected.

Having used the word "always," we now have to point out the exceptions to the rule. When using CI in large, complex systems, you may have to break the build into smaller pieces to reduce the amount of time required. Breaking down the build based on module relationships and dependencies ensures that your team builds and tests all code affected by a change.

For example, consider a financial system that contains modules for managing user account information and tracking the stock market, as in Figure 5-1. The two modules interact with a database that drives the system's user interface. A system this small probably doesn't warrant breaking the build into pieces, but it is useful for demonstrating how to apply CI to large, complex systems effectively.

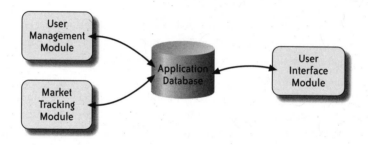

FIGURE 5-1. Part of a financial system

To break the build into smaller pieces, start by looking for independent modules. The user management and market tracking modules are completely decoupled, so they are candidates for separate builds. Changes to the user management module don't affect the market tracking module. Likewise, changes to the market tracking module don't affect the user management module. The decoupled modules may be built separately; however, both modules may indirectly affect the user interface via the database, so you should build (and test) the user interface module as part of both builds, as in Figure 5-2.

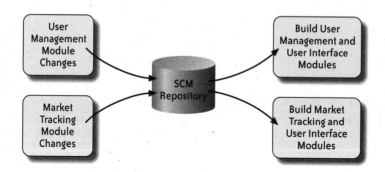

FIGURE 5-2. Separate builds for decoupled modules

End-to-End Builds

CI builds are end-to-end processes. End-to-end builds start from source code and include all the actions necessary to create the final software product. The definitions of "all the actions necessary" and "final software product" are arbitrary, and different development teams may apply different meanings to each. For example, the simplest end-to-end build consists of nothing more than compiling source code into an executable file, as shown in Figure 5-3.

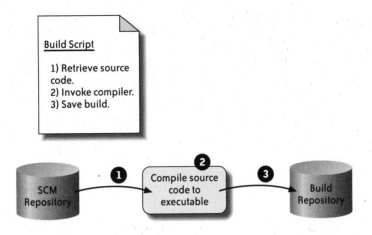

FIGURE 5-3. Simple end-to-end build

While a simple end-to-end build implements a repeatable process for creating executables, it doesn't incorporate all the steps typically performed prior to releasing a software product. CI builds are often more complex and may include:

- Unit and integration testing
- Database initialization
- Code coverage analysis
- Coding standards inspections
- Performance and load testing
- Documentation generation
- Packaging of executables into deployable products
- Automatic deployment of products

Figure 5-4 shows a typical end-to-end build used in a CI process, including automatic deployment of the product. Be aware that automatic deployment is a tricky proposition. Updating a product while it is being tested or used can cause confusion and can result in decreased productivity, lost data, and a lack of confidence in the product.

Builds resulting in deployable software packages are sometimes referred to as *push button builds* because a single command creates the entire product from scratch. Builds that are started automatically at preset times are called *scheduled builds*.

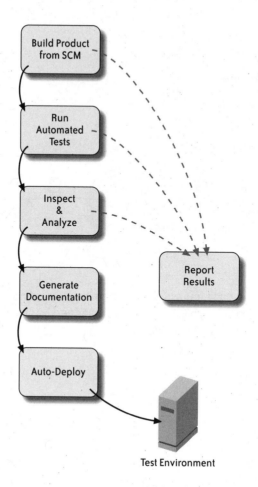

FIGURE 5-4. Typical end-to-end build

Reporting Results

CI builds employ automated reporting mechanisms to ensure that developers, managers, and possibly even customers always know the state of the build. Report content depends on the complexity of the build; simple builds may report compiler errors, whereas more complex builds may include error messages, unit and integration test results, code coverage statistics, adherence to standards, and statistics generated by performance testing.

An important part of the process is getting reports to developers quickly. Broken builds disrupt the normal flow of development because developers working on other parts of the system can't use the latest version of source code from SCM. The sooner the developers who are responsible for the bad code know the build is broken, the sooner they can fix it and restore the flow.

Results can be reported in a number of different ways. Some of the more common methods are:

Email notifications
> Build failures generate email notifications to the development team, alerting everyone that the build is broken and needs attention. The first build to pass after a failure also generates an email notification, giving the "all clear" signal.

RSS feeds
> Really Simple Syndication (RSS) feeds are handy ways to display the build status continually. Feeds can be viewed via a generic RSS reader or a custom application, allowing developers to see the current build status at a glance.

Web pages
> Web pages are another handy way to continually display build status. Many of the software packages used to implement CI include a web application that tracks and displays the status automatically, allowing anyone to see the status simply by viewing a web page.

Physical indicators
> Physical indicators, such as red and green lights, can be used to indicate build status. Although they don't provide details, physical indicators do display the current status in an easily interpreted way.

Dedicated Build Servers

Many CI gurus insist on using a dedicated machine for performing builds. Often referred to as *build servers*, these machines provide a number of benefits, but they also have some drawbacks. Whether you implement CI with or without a dedicated build server depends on your situation.

Dedicated Build Servers Isolate Build Activities

Using a dedicated build server prevents interference from other activities. Other activities may slow down or even halt a build due to limited resources or access issues.

The primary function of a build server is to build and test the project. Build servers doing double duty, such as hosting the test database for a web application or hosting the web server itself, will require more time to build the software. Small projects with few developers may be able to utilize a less powerful machine or allow the machine to perform other tasks without sacrificing build speed. However, large projects with many developers and frequent code check-ins will benefit from having a powerful, dedicated build server.

Dedicated Build Servers Provide a Well-Known Build Environment Configuration

Dedicated build servers allow you to build and test the product in a well-known environment. Users performing other tasks on a shared build server may load different versions of libraries and supporting software or make changes to the runtime or test environment resulting in build failures.

Build servers should not be used for prototyping, experimenting with new technologies, or evaluating new software packages. Each of these activities can introduce new versions of libraries and make system-level configuration changes that are incompatible with the build environment.

Dedicated Build Servers Require Extra Hardware

One drawback of using a dedicated build server is the expense of obtaining an additional computer, one that will not be used by developers for writing code. In addition, you may require a fairly powerful machine to deal with large, complex builds.

Setting up a dedicated build server requires an initial investment, but the payoff is well worth the expense. One of the main drivers behind CI is immediate feedback, so the more powerful the machine, the better. Faster builds mean faster feedback to developers. If at all possible, consider using a powerful, dedicated build server to implement CI.

Continuous Integration Software

CI software applications, also known as CI servers, must do three things to control the CI process: detect changes in the SCM repository, invoke build scripts, and report results.

CI Servers Detect Changes in the SCM Repository

Because CI is based on rebuilding the system whenever the codebase changes, it requires the capability to detect such changes automatically. CI servers typically include the capability to interface with a wide variety of SCM systems, allowing them to monitor the repository and take action when the codebase changes, or to defer action when no changes are detected.

CI Servers Invoke Build Scripts

Once a CI server has detected a change in the codebase, it starts an automated build process by invoking a build script. Typically, CI servers incorporate a mechanism to ensure that all pending changes to the SCM repository are completed before invoking the build script. Once it has started the build script, the CI server monitors the process and waits for it to finish.

CI Servers Report Build Results

The final responsibility of a CI server is to report the build results to the development team and anyone else who needs to know the build status. CI servers commonly provide error notification via email and web-based access to the latest build results.

CI Servers Can Schedule Builds

A strict interpretation of CI does not include scheduled builds, but such builds can be useful in managing large, complex products. Using a combination of builds triggered by code changes and scheduled builds, developers can create a system that performs fast-running unit and integration tests for all code changes and longer tests in the background. Most CI servers allow you to schedule builds for a particular time of day—a nightly build, for example—or on a periodic basis.

Implementing Continuous Integration

As we mentioned at the beginning of the chapter, CI is the process of continually integrating small code changes into a software product. Each time the codebase changes (i.e., changes are checked into the SCM repository), the system is built and tested. Developers are notified immediately of any errors caused by the changes, allowing them to make corrections quickly. CI can be thought of as an extension of automated builds in that it performs an automated build (including testing, reporting, and other actions) each time the codebase changes.

So, you've decided to implement CI on your project. What do you do first? Start with the first three prerequisites noted at the beginning of the chapter. If you've been following this book's recommendations about the order in which to implement practices, you should already have two of the three completed (SCM and automated testing). If not, refer to the appropriate practices in the preceding chapters. These prerequisites are:

1. Establish an SCM repository for all source code, scripts, test data, etc. Just about any modern SCM system will do, although several have gained wide acceptance in the industry.
2. Identify a build server. Ensure that the server has access to the SCM repository.
3. Identify the unit testing framework(s) necessary to support unit testing the project. Load the framework software onto the build server.

If you've already implemented automated builds using a build scripting language, you're done with the next step. If not, work through the following list to establish an automated build script for your project:

1. Choose a build scripting language that supports the SCM software and unit testing framework you'll be using.
2. Load the scripting software onto the build server.
3. Create a simple build script that retrieves all source code from the SCM repository.
4. Add a compile task to the build script for each module in the project.
5. *Add the build script to the SCM repository!*

One way to create the compile task for each module is to copy the script that has been created for the module by an integrated development environment (IDE), such as Eclipse or Microsoft Visual Studio. A parent script can pull the individual scripts together and invoke them in order to perform the complete build. In many cases, you can use IDEs in a command-line mode, allowing the CI process to invoke the IDE to perform the build directly.

With a build script for each module in place, it's time to create the CI process itself. Here we assume you'll be using one of the available CI servers:

1. Select a CI server with the features and compatibilities you need (SCM, build scripting language, and unit test framework).
2. Load the CI server software onto the build machine.
3. Configure the CI server to monitor the project's SCM repository and to execute the master build script when changes are detected.
4. Start the CI server.

Virtually all CI servers have the ability to monitor the repository for changes, so once started, the CI server should initiate a build whenever any changes are made to the SCM repository.

Now that the CI server is building the project, we need to report the results. The next step is to add a reporting mechanism to the CI process. Results are typically reported by adding tasks to the build script. The tasks may generate XML data in a particular format for display in a web application, generate emails to developers when something fails, set the state of a visual indicator, or update an RSS feed. Select the desired reporting mechanism and add it as appropriate for the CI server in use.

The CI process is now on the verge of doing something useful. All that's left is to add unit testing and report the results. As with reporting mechanisms, unit testing is typically invoked from within the build script. Modifying the build script to invoke all existing unit tests makes it easier to add modules (as well as unit tests for legacy code) later. New unit tests will be picked up automatically as they are added to the SCM repository.

At this point, the project has a working, useful CI process that will build the project when changes are detected in the repository and will notify developers if the build or unit tests fail. You can enhance the CI process to include other tasks such as code analysis, load testing, documentation, and deployment by adding the appropriate task to the build script.

Developers and the CI Process

An effective CI process requires more than a collection of tools and scripts; it requires acceptance by the development team members. CI works by integrating small pieces of functionality at regular intervals. Developers must adhere to a few rules to make the CI process effective:

Frequent check-ins

Developers should check code into the SCM repository at least once a day, preferably several times a day. The longer modified code remains checked out, the more likely it is to get out of sync with the rest of the project, leading to problems integrating the code when it is finally checked in.

Only check in functional code

Although code should be checked in often, it should not be checked in if it is not yet functional, doesn't compile, or fails unit tests. Developers must build the updated project locally and run the applicable unit tests before checking code into the repository.

The highest priority task is fixing build failures

When a failure is detected in the build, fixing the failure becomes the highest priority. Allowing a build failure to persist adds the risk of integration problems to ongoing development, so developers need to focus on fixing the problem before moving forward.

Continuous Integration Builds Quality in

CI benefits a software development organization in a number of ways. All of the descriptions that follow assume the CI implementation includes a robust set of unit and integration tests that are run each time the source code is rebuilt.

Aid Debugging by Limiting the Scope of Errors

An effective CI implementation requires users to check changes into SCM frequently. Frequent check-ins tend to limit both the size and scope of changes, which in turn limit the possible sources of error when a test fails. CI helps speed debugging by limiting the source of a test failure to recent changes.

Provide Immediate Feedback for Changes

Feedback for changes is not limited to test failures; it includes successful integrations as well. CI provides both positive and negative feedback about recent changes, allowing developers to see the effects of those changes quickly. The negative or positive quality of those effects can then drive additional changes or a determination that no more work is required.

Minimize Integration Effort

Traditional software development life cycles include an integration phase sandwiched between the end of development and the release of the product. CI minimizes—and sometimes eliminates completely—the integration phase. By spreading the integration effort out over the entire development cycle, CI allows developers to integrate smaller changes. Integrating smaller changes frequently doesn't simply spread the same effort out over a longer period; it actually reduces the integration effort. Because the changes are small and limited to specific sections of the source code, isolation of errors is quicker and debugging is easier.

Minimize Propagation of Defects

An undetected defect in one module can propagate through the software system via dependencies with other modules. When the defect is finally discovered, the fix affects not only the defective module, but also all modules dependent on it. First, the defect propagates through the system, and then the fix propagates through the system.

Continuous integration minimizes the propagation of defects through the system by detecting the problem early (via thorough automated unit and integration testing), before it has a chance to propagate.

Create a Safety Net for Developers

A significant part of any development effort involves modifying existing code to account for changing requirements and refactoring modules to improve the overall software implementation. Developers can modify and refactor code with confidence because CI is providing a safety net. The unit and integration tests that run as part of the build give immediate feedback to developers, who can roll back changes if something causes the build to break.

Ensure the Latest and Greatest Software Is Always Available

Because CI builds the project whenever the code changes, it keeps the latest build in sync with the code repository. A CI implementation that reads from an SCM repository and deploys the build to a test environment ensures that developers, testers, and users are all working with the latest version of software.

Provide a Snapshot of the Current State of the Project

Because CI reports the state of every build, it provides up-to-date visibility into the current state of the project. The snapshot may include:

- Results of the latest build, which tells developers what needs to be fixed before moving forward.
- Metrics resulting from unit testing, code coverage, and coding standards analysis, which allows team leaders to gauge the team's adherence to processes.
- Number of passing tests, which indicates how many requirements are actually completed and can provide managers with insight into the progress of the project.

Resistance to Implementing CI

Much of the resistance to implementing CI has to do with increased cost in terms of time, money, or both. Some has to do with retrofitting CI onto a system not designed to support it. In most cases, the benefits outweigh the costs; however, being aware of the arguments against CI will help prepare you to convince management it's a good idea.

CI Requires Extra Hardware

As discussed earlier in the section "Dedicated Build Servers," CI works best with a powerful computer dedicated to performing builds and all the associated tasks. Although CI can be implemented without a dedicated build server, the benefits generally outweigh the costs of extra hardware, even when the machine is a very powerful (i.e., expensive) one. Even so, there are at least two ways to get started with CI on something less than the biggest, fastest machine on the market: piggyback on an existing server or use a less powerful machine that no one wants.

Piggybacking on an existing server or shared computer, such as a test machine or an underutilized web server, is a quick way to implement CI. Such machines are often already running the typical deployment environment, so you only have to load the CI-related software. When following this approach, the more stable the environment, the better. A server whose configuration is changed often will lead to inconsistent build results.

Implementing CI on a less powerful machine—perhaps one left over from the last time the development machines were upgraded—provides the benefits of a dedicated machine at the cost of fast builds. Whether a less powerful machine is adequate for a particular project will depend on a number of factors, such as the number of developers and the frequency of check-ins (both directly affect the frequency of builds), the size of the build, and the number and type of automated tests. Less powerful machines may be enough for small development efforts. Larger, more complex projects can use this approach to demonstrate the benefits of CI in an effort to lobby management for the funds to obtain a more powerful machine.

Both of these approaches can provide a starting point for implementing CI, but there is no substitute for a powerful, dedicated build server. In the end, the justification is simply that the time saved during integration far outweighs the upfront costs of adequate hardware.

CI Requires New Software

Though it is possible to implement CI from scratch with custom scripts and applications, the easiest approach is to use a third-party CI server application, many of which are available as open source software. Implementing CI with open source packages can reduce the initial cost to almost nothing, although there are maintenance and training costs to consider. Other software packages required for implementing CI—such as an SCM system, a build scripting language, and a unit test framework—are also available as open source software.

As with most software, there is a learning curve associated with CI software; however, CI software packages are usually independent of the project software, so experience gained on one project transfers easily to new projects. In addition, you can implement CI in a stepwise fashion, starting simply and enhancing the process as developers learn more about the package.

CI Adds Maintenance Tasks

In addition to the initial setup tasks, CI requires ongoing maintenance of the build scripts, although the amount of ongoing maintenance is fairly small. This type of maintenance typically involves creating build scripts for new modules and adding tasks to the build process.

Creating the build script for a new module can be time-consuming, since you must take care to ensure that all dependencies are accounted for and all required libraries are available. As noted earlier, one way to simplify the task is to use an IDE to create a build script that can be invoked by the CI process.

Spending time upfront to organize the project structure (in conjunction with the SCM repository structure) and create extensible build scripts often reduces work necessary for both the addition of tasks and the addition of modules. You can add tasks to the build script such that they apply to all modules or a specific subset of them. And good build scripts will automatically incorporate repository changes, so adding and deleting modules is as simple as adding or removing the module from the SCM repository.

CI for Legacy Code Is Expensive

Continuous integration is most effective when used with a robust set of unit tests; after all, without testing, CI degrades to simply compilation of the source code. Legacy code often lacks unit tests (at least automated unit tests), so retrofitting CI onto an existing project can be a daunting task.

The best approach to implementing CI in a legacy system is to begin by creating build scripts for the existing modules, including any unit tests that exist. Unit tests are then added to legacy modules as the modules are modified or refactored, expanding unit test coverage to the entire legacy codebase over time. New modules are required to have unit tests before being allowed into the build. Chapter 4 covers the implementation of unit tests for legacy code in detail.

Summary

CI is the process of integrating small changes at short intervals. The process reduces, and sometimes eliminates, the need for an integration phase at the end of development. CI involves building the entire software product, testing it, and reporting the results whenever changes are made, which provides immediate feedback to the developers responsible for the changes.

The CI process has several prerequisites, though these prerequisites are themselves valid practices for implementing Lean and Agile methodologies. You can implement CI gradually, starting with a basic build and unit test sequence and expanding to include automated integration and acceptance testing, code analysis, and even deployment.

The benefits of a well-implemented CI process include detecting defects as soon as possible, minimizing the propagation of defects, simplifying the debug process by limiting the scope of errors, minimizing the integration phase, providing immediate feedback to developers, and raising the visibility of the project's status. These benefits are gained at the expense of an initial setup process, additional hardware and software, and, possibly, a change in the way developers handle source code and automated testing.

CHAPTER SIX

Practice 3: Less Code

There is nothing so useless as doing efficiently that which should not be done at all.

—Peter Drucker

Don't panic. We're not trying to put you out of a job. "Less code" isn't about writing less software; it's about getting the job done with fewer lines of code. It's about eliminating unnecessary code and making the necessary code more efficient. It's about keeping the codebase small while still delivering functionality (and thus value) to the customer.

Codebase size affects projects in several ways, the most obvious of which is the amount of time required to write the code. More lines of code mean more time spent writing them. But code size has farther-reaching effects as well, since larger codebases:

- Typically mean more components, which in turn mean more connections between components and more integration effort.
- Mean more errors, which mean longer bug lists and more debugging.
- Are more difficult to understand, increasing the learning curve for new developers and for future maintenance efforts.
- Have more "inertia," which makes it more difficult to respond to change.

As large codebases drive more components, more bugs, and longer learning curves, they drive up both development and maintenance costs. The definition of waste in Lean development is anything that increases costs without providing value, so the costs resulting from developing and maintaining unnecessarily large codebases can be viewed as waste.

Writing less code requires developers to adopt an attitude that looks critically at every line of code. Minimizing the size of a codebase, however, isn't limited to implementation. Every aspect of development affects the amount of code written, so developers must apply a minimalist attitude throughout the entire development process.

Traditional software development methods encourage customers to create complete sets of requirements upfront. When told that it is more expensive to make requirements changes later in the development cycle, customers create requirements for everything they can think of. In Chapter 2, we presented the results of the CHAOS study, which showed that 45% of developed features are never used by the customer. Eliminating the requirements that drive development of unused features can significantly reduce the codebase size.

Instead of this "kitchen sink" approach to writing requirements, which focuses on speculation instead of known needs and leads to unused features, requirements should be built up over time. Initial requirements should be based on real needs, not imagination. The full requirements list can be created and refined incrementally as both customers and developers gain a better understanding of the problem and solution.

Designs that are flexible enough to accommodate future changes and additions can be huge timesavers, but designs that account for every possibility lead to unused code and bloated interfaces. Like kitchen-sink requirements, overly flexible designs focus on speculation instead of what's really needed to provide immediate value. Trading upfront design for emergent design (evolving the design to account for emerging needs) leads to systems that are both flexible and efficient. Scott Bain's book, *Emergent Design: The Evolutionary Nature of*

Professional Software Development (Addison-Wesley Professional), provides an in-depth discussion of emergent design in software development.

A complete set of unit tests is critical to the development process (see Chapter 4); unit tests add value by building quality into the system and reducing long-term maintenance costs. However, developing unit tests for unnecessary code is piling waste on top of waste. As with all other code in the codebase, time and effort are required to write, debug, maintain, and execute unit tests, and none of that time and effort adds value to the final product when the code is unnecessary in the first place.

Scope creep is a common phenomenon in software development. Customers can be counted on to change their minds and think of new features, and developers have a natural tendency to anticipate future changes and plan ahead for them. New requirements are inevitable and flexible designs are desirable, but allowing them to occur unchecked can lead to bloated interfaces and unneeded code.

The rest of the chapter delves deeper into techniques for minimizing the size of a project's codebase. We discuss principles that build a minimalist approach to development, we describe actual techniques to realize those principles, and we look at some of the problems you're likely to encounter as you attempt to minimize your codebase.

Leaning out the Codebase

An overweight, out-of-shape person who wants to become a healthy, fit person needs to do three things: diet, get in shape, and maintain healthy habits over time. The same is true of any codebase, as shown in Figure 6-1. To trim the size of a codebase and keep it small, we have to eliminate unnecessary code, employ good coding practices, and justify any new code.

Eliminate Unnecessary Code

The easiest way to reduce the codebase size is to eliminate unnecessary code. Any code that doesn't directly support existing requirements is unnecessary, as are unit tests for that code. Examples of unnecessary code include class interfaces with multiple overloaded methods (are 10 different constructors really necessary?), overuse or early implementation of design patterns (a factory pattern creating only one type of object is overkill), and "nice to have" features that the customer hasn't requested.

Of course, there are times when anticipating future needs is an integral part of the software being developed (a framework application developed specifically to allow extension via plug-ins must provide flexible interfaces) or when removing unused code from a legacy application is more effort than it's worth. Just as a diet of bread and water may accomplish the goal of losing weight to the point of malnutrition, eliminating code can be taken too far. You should combine careful analysis with common sense and a reasonable view of the future of the system to determine what code is unnecessary.

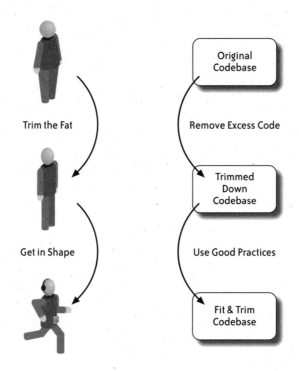

FIGURE 6-1. *Writing less code is a fitness program*

Undertaking a campaign to eliminate all unnecessary code from an existing codebase can have a detrimental effect on continuing development. There are two approaches that you can use to trim the codebase over time and minimize this effect. The first approach is similar to adding unit tests to legacy code: apply "less code" principles to legacy code when the code is changed for some other reason, such as fixing a defect or changing existing functionality. The second approach is to eliminate unnecessary code only when the cost of maintaining it into the future exceeds the cost of rewriting it now.

Employ Good Coding Practices

The epigraph opening this chapter points out that efficient effort is a poor substitute for eliminating effort completely, but that is not an excuse for ignoring efficiency. Both are required to achieve a truly minimal codebase. Good coding practices hone the codebase, making it smaller, more efficient, and more understandable.

Justify All New Code

Once the code is trimmed down and in shape, keep it that way. Maintaining a small codebase requires applying the first two principles to any new code. Only add new code if it directly supports current requirements, and ensure the new code adheres to defined best practices. Code that exists only to support anticipated changes or features doesn't make the cut, nor does bloated, inefficient code. Losing weight and getting in shape are only half the battle; keeping the weight off and staying in shape requires life-long diligence.

Developing Less Code

The principles we have just described and the techniques that follow lead to smaller codebases and should be applied right from the start of a project. Keeping a codebase small is much easier than reducing the size of an existing codebase. And while legacy code presents a more difficult problem, it can also benefit from some of the techniques employed to minimize code. As with automated testing, you can reduce the size of a legacy codebase incrementally, applying the principles as the legacy code is changed for other reasons.

Several techniques exist for implementing the "less code" principles. Prioritizing requirements, developing in short iterations, developing only for the current iteration, avoiding unnecessary complexity, and reuse can all help to eliminate unnecessary code. Coding standards, best practices, design patterns, and refactoring can all help to make code more efficient.

Prioritize Requirements

A rule of thumb that is often applied to customer requirements is the "80/20" rule (mentioned earlier in Chapter 2). The 80/20 rule states that:

> 80% of the useful functionality of a software application is described by 20% of the requirements.

By implementing the most significant 20% of the requirements, a development team can implement 80% of the functionality required by the customer. Prioritizing requirements makes it clear which features constitute that 20% and allows developers to concentrate on those features.

Requirements are often written to include everything a customer can think of—after all, we've been telling them for years that it costs more to make changes later than to specify things upfront. Eighty percent of those requirements will be features that provide little value to the end user. If the development team treats all requirements equally, a lot of code will be written to implement features the customer doesn't really care about. In other words, a lot of unnecessary code may be added to the codebase.

How does prioritization minimize the size of the codebase? When combined with short, frequent iterations, it drives the team to develop the most important features early and gives the customer a chance to stop the development when existing code is "good enough" or when features are deemed unnecessary. The code to implement unused features is never written.

PRIORITIZED REQUIREMENTS

Prioritized requirements are a recurring theme in Lean software development. In particular, they facilitate minimizing codebase size and the use of short iterations (see Chapter 7). More generally, they ensure that developers are creating the right product by providing a road map of the features considered most important by the customer.

Prioritized requirements also play a role in reducing waste. The highest priority features are likely to be those the customer understands the best and is least likely to change, so implementing them first minimizes the risk that development effort will be wasted.

Effective prioritization of requirements relies on the priorities being dynamic. Customer feedback often drives changes to the requirements in the form of added, deleted, and modified requirements. Also, as the product begins to take shape, customers gain a better understanding of what the product should do and how to use it in the deployed environment. The changing shape of the product changes the importance of specific features, and those changes must be reflected in the requirements prioritization.

You should keep several key concepts in mind when prioritizing requirements:

- Base priorities on value to the customer. This means that the customer must be involved in the process. Developers should not prioritize requirements directly. Although their estimates of the development effort for a given feature may influence the customer, it is the customer who decides what is most important.

- Reevaluate priorities often. Start each iteration with a freshly prioritized list to ensure that you incorporate changes in customer needs.

- Requirements should be individually prioritized, not simply set to "high," "medium," or "low." Unique numeric priorities force customers to objectively evaluate their needs, and they eliminate ambiguity when selecting which requirements to include in an iteration.

Develop in Short Iterations

Short iterations are discussed fully in Chapter 7, so here we will mention simply that they are a hallmark of Agile development methodologies and directly support the Lean principles of eliminating waste, deferring commitment, and delivering quickly. Short iterations deliver new functionality to customers quickly and frequently, shortening the delivery and feedback cycle and reducing the time that developers and customers wait for one another.

Develop Only for the Current Iteration

Developing for the current iteration, which uses a prioritized list of requirements and short iterations, helps minimize the codebase by focusing development on the requirements that are most important to the customer. Assuming a prioritized list of requirements for the current iteration exists (see the earlier sidebar on prioritized requirements), the criteria for implementing a design aspect or a feature also exist: only code that directly supports the requirements assigned to the current iteration is developed. Maintaining a focus on the current iteration ensures that the highest priority features are implemented and that developers are not sidetracked by adding extra features. Essentially, developing for only the current iteration means, "If it isn't needed right now, don't do it." However, as we'll see in the next section, things are not always so straightforward.

Avoid Unnecessary Complexity

Two topics guaranteed to generate heated discussions are YAGNI (You Ain't Gonna Need It) and BDUF (Big Design Up Front). Ron Jeffries defines YAGNI this way:

> Always implement things when you actually need them, never when you just foresee that you need them.

The YAGNI principle is based on the unpredictability of tomorrow's requirements. Proponents of YAGNI claim that implementing features (or design elements) now based on what may be needed later has a number of drawbacks, including:

- Implementing features based on anticipated needs creates the risk of wasting development effort on features that may be discarded when the needs fail to materialize.

- Unneeded features incur support costs (i.e., testing, debugging, documentation) without providing value to the customer.

- Implementing unneeded features takes development time away from the features that are needed, slowing the delivery of usable software to customers.

- Attempting to anticipate all the uses of a feature or design results in code bloat.

BDUF, often regarded as a holdover from the Waterfall development methodology, is characterized by a separate design phase where a complete design is constructed before any code is written. Most Agile methodologies dismiss a separate design phase as detrimental to flexibility, claiming that upfront design is unrealistic on any nontrivial project and that the rigidity imposed by such a design is in direct opposition to flexibility.

Taken to extremes, these two ideas are diametrically opposed: YAGNI says to create it as you need it; BDUF says to define it all ahead of time. From an Agile perspective, YAGNI would seem to be the right approach, but things aren't quite that simple. YAGNI detractors say it leads to inefficient designs and rework due to a lack of a "big picture" and YAGNI's assumption that you cannot foresee future needs is needlessly myopic. BDUF supporters hold it up as the solution to YAGNI's shortcomings, claiming it results in more efficient designs and ensures all requirements are implemented.

At first glance, the approaches seem incompatible; however, when we look closer, an opportunity for compromise appears. The compromise takes the best aspects of each approach and combines them with a dash of common sense. Invoke YAGNI where it's appropriate, but temper it with some foresight about what's in store in future iterations. Do some design up front, honestly evaluating what's really needed and what's speculation, and then allow the design to evolve as features are added. Remember, the idea is to avoid *unnecessary* complexity, not to replace complexity with brute force arbitrarily. Employ YAGNI, BDUF, and a little common sense to keep the code both flexible and efficient.

Reuse Existing Software

One of the most effective ways to write less code is to reuse existing software; it maximizes functionality while minimizing codebase size. It also directly addresses each of the problems inherent in large codebases, since reuse reduces:

- Coding time by decreasing the amount of code written.
- The number of components, though not necessarily the number of connections between components.
- Debugging by adding functionality that is already using debugged code.
- Learning curves by limiting the number of different components a developer must understand.

Software reuse exists in many different forms, each of which affects codebase size differently:

- Copying source code from one component to another reduces coding time and debugging, but it actually increases codebase size.
- Modular components and plug-ins allow you to write code once and reuse it multiple times to reduce the amount of source code.
- Services that are hosted in a Service-Oriented Architecture (SOA) system minimize the codebase size by allowing developers to use existing functionality.
- Libraries and frameworks provide built-in functionality.

Although you must consider issues such as applicability of existing components, long-term availability of services, and licensing and distribution fees for third-party software, reusing existing software is a valid approach to writing less code.

Use Coding Standards and Best Practices

Coding standards help developers create an easily understandable codebase. They shorten the learning curve for developers who need to work on code they did not write themselves, and they allow developers to spend less time figuring out the quirks of another developer's coding style and more time figuring out what the code does.

Every programming language and development environment has its own coding standard, and most have more than one. Although some of the rules in a given standard are arbitrary and reflect the personal preferences of the author, many rules are consistent from standard to standard. Moreover, standards can be modified to fit a particular development team or project. In the end, using a coding standard is more important than which standard is selected.

Best practices take the concept of coding standards a step further and can help you avoid common errors and reduce complexity. They give developers guidance on using language features correctly and, like coding standards, they help developers understand each other's code.

A blurry line separates coding standards and best practices, but they both support "less code" principles. They create a common language (above and beyond the programming language) that allows developers to understand each other's code, and they reduce complexity by describing the best way to implement specific coding constructs.

Analysis applications exist for coding standards and best practices for many programming languages and development environments. You can combine these applications with continuous integration (Chapter 5) to automatically enforce the chosen standards and practices.

Use Design Patterns

Design patterns are general solutions to recurring problems. They solve common problems in various contexts by reusing the general structure of a known solution and altering it as necessary to fit the situation. In a sense, patterns are standards and best practices applied to design.

Design patterns focus on improving a system's design; however, implementing solutions with design patterns generates several side effects that reduce the size of the codebase, such as removing duplication, simplifying design, using advanced language features to implement object interactions implicitly, and creating reusable components.

Although design patterns can be appropriate when using upfront design in limited amounts, they are most effective in Lean software development as a way to evolve a design over time. The evolution of a design occurs as functionality is added over several iterations and the design is refactored to accommodate it. As the implementation grows and elements of design patterns emerge, you can refactor the design as instantiations of the emerging patterns.

Refactor Code and Design

Refactoring is the process of modifying the internal implementation of a component without changing the public interface or behavior of the component. Within the context of writing less code, the goal of refactoring is to reduce the amount of code by modifying the implementation to take advantage of known solutions. Known solutions to common problems typically have been refined over time into efficient implementations, whether at the basic coding level (best practices) or at the design level (design patterns).

Refactoring can help reduce the size of the codebase by taking advantage of known solutions. However, to be effective, refactoring must be a regular part of the implementation effort. Individual developers must make refactoring at the code level part of their daily routine: first, implement a requirement as a simple, even brute-force, solution, and then refactor the solution to make it as efficient as possible. Refactoring at the design level requires coordination between developers as the elements of design patterns emerge. Often, a senior developer assumes the role of architect, reviewing the implementation for emerging designs on a regular basis.

Resistance to "Less Code"

You are likely to meet with some resistance when implementing the practices described here, primarily from the more experienced members of the development team. The practices usually require developers to change the way they write code; after all, if they're already writing code this way, there's no need to change anything.

When developers are used to writing all their own code, they often develop a distrust of third-party software as well. Overcoming the "not invented here" attitude can be difficult, especially with more experienced developers who have had bad experiences with such software in the past. In addition, libraries and frameworks may come with licensing and distribution fees that make them a more expensive option initially.

Coding standards and best practices cause developers to change the way they write code, and even the most junior members of the team will have their own preferences. The best approach may be to pick one of the industry standards for the language and development environment of choice. Any changes to that standard then have to be agreed upon by the entire team. Minor formatting issues often can be eliminated through the use of code-formatting applications that reformat code as it is checked into the SCM repository.

Effective refactoring of code and design requires knowledge and experience, though this really isn't a valid reason to avoid it. One way to enhance developers' refactoring skills is to encourage practicing. Practice sessions should be conducted outside of the actual development effort, which means they will take some time away from that effort; however, the benefit is well worth the cost. In a practice session, developers refactor code using established techniques. At the end of the practice session, the refactored code is thrown away, not checked into the SCM repository. Throwing away the practice code encourages developers to try new approaches and experiment with techniques to see what works without the threat of breaking anything in the production codebase. Martin Fowler's book, *Refactoring: Improving the Design of Existing Code* (Addison-Wesley Professional), is an excellent starting point. Also, many development environments have refactoring capabilities built in.

Learning the design patterns targeted by refactoring at the design level may take upfront training and ongoing study to be effective. Design patterns can make code more efficient, but the misuse of design patterns can unnecessarily increase the complexity of the software. Be prepared to arrange training for developers who are unfamiliar with the use of design patterns.

Management may provide some resistance when working with legacy code. Removing unused code seems unnecessary since it isn't affecting the product, and refactoring the working code sounds a lot like rewriting to most managers. However, by applying "less code" principles only to code that must be modified for other reasons, and doing so only when it is cost-effective, you can address legacy code without an extensive rewriting effort.

Summary

Large codebases drive up development and maintenance costs by requiring more time to create and debug, and by creating longer learning curves for developers. When this cost is incurred while creating unneeded or unused code, it is waste because it doesn't deliver value to the customer.

All aspects of software development—from requirements definition to design, implementation, and tests—contribute to codebase size. Minimizing the codebase size requires developers to be aware of the impact from each of these areas, and to look critically at anything that increases the amount of code.

Minimizing a codebase, whether it is a legacy system or a new development effort, is like a physical fitness program. First, you have to go on a diet to lose weight (eliminate unnecessary code); next, you have to hit the gym to get in shape (employ good coding practices); and finally, you have to maintain weight and fitness level (look critically at anything that has a chance of increasing the codebase).

Prioritized requirements are an important part of minimizing the codebase size, and they play a part in many other aspects of Lean and Agile software development.

It takes time and effort to instill the habits that help reduce the amount of code. Developers must learn new ways to approach writing code, and they will need to practice those techniques. Expect some resistance.

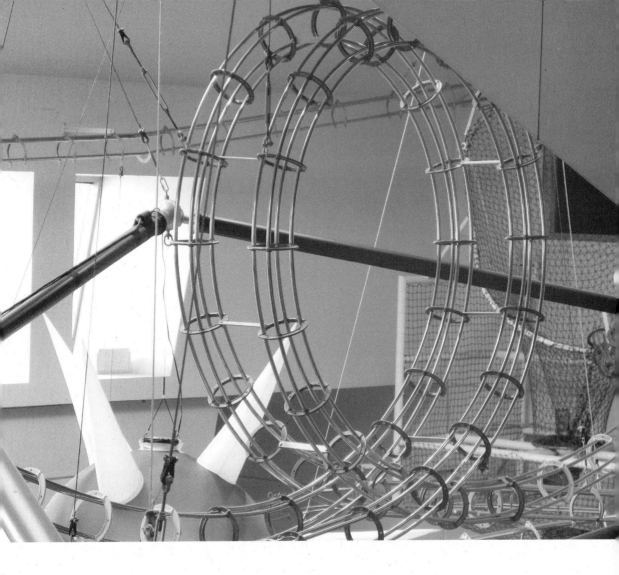

CHAPTER SEVEN

Practice 4: Short Iterations

He doubly benefits the needy who gives quickly.

—Publilius Syrus

Iterative development delivers functional software to the customer for evaluation at specific intervals. Each iteration adds new functionality to the product and increases the customer's understanding of how the final product will fulfill his needs. It also provides an opportunity to identify how the product may fall short. The effectiveness of iterative development comes from these opportunities to receive and incorporate customer feedback. Customer feedback drives the next iteration by adding, deleting, and modifying requirements to correct shortcomings, and iteration length determines the number of opportunities available during a development effort. This means that short iterations provide more feedback and increase the possibility that the final product will be what the customer wants.

Short iterations support three of the Lean software development principles described in Chapter 2:

- Eliminate waste
- Defer commitment
- Deliver fast

Two forms of waste that are prevalent in software development are partially completed work and replanning. Partially completed work is any work that has been started but not completed; it includes such things as uncoded requirements and incomplete, untested code. Because partially completed work doesn't contribute new functionality to the current product, it is non-value-added work. In addition, if the customer decides to stop development, in a specific area or for the entire product, any partially completed work is wasted effort. Planning too far into the future can result in replanning when the customer's needs change. Effort spent in the initial planning is wasted when work is replanned. Short iterations prevent both situations by focusing efforts on developing the customer's highest priority requirements quickly and planning just far enough ahead to support that development.

Deferring commitment means putting off irrevocable decisions as long as possible (and reasonable). Delaying such decisions gives developers time to gather the information needed to make them, and short iterations provide opportunities to collect that information in the form of customer feedback. Developers can create prototypes of the final implementation in an early iteration, gather feedback, and use the feedback to decide on the final implementation in a later iteration.

As noted earlier, iterative development puts new functionality in the customer's hands at specific intervals. Short iterations support the "deliver fast" principle by reducing interval size and delivering new functionality in quick response to customer feedback. Instead of waiting until the final delivery of the product to see the effects of their comments, customers see it in the next iteration.

The use of short iterations in Lean software development relies on both underlying principles and specific techniques for implementing those principles.

Short Iterations Generate Customer Value

Two major principles drive the use of short iterations in Lean software development: increasing feedback opportunities and making course corrections. Getting feedback from the customer and implementing that feedback allow you to develop the product efficiently, get the product delivered quickly, and ensure the final product supports the customer's needs.

Increase Feedback Opportunities

One of the goals of short iterations is to increase the amount of feedback received from the customer. Short iterations deliver new functionality more often, thus increasing the number of opportunities customers have to evaluate the product. Figure 7-1 shows graphically how shorter iterations increase feedback opportunities. A 12-month development effort consisting of a single iteration provides no opportunity for feedback until after the final product is delivered, at which point it's too late. Breaking the effort into two iterations provides some feedback, allowing developers to modify software developed during the first six months in the second six months. But if a little feedback is good, more should be better, right? By breaking the development into monthly iterations, developers can get feedback from customers at 11 points during the development effort.

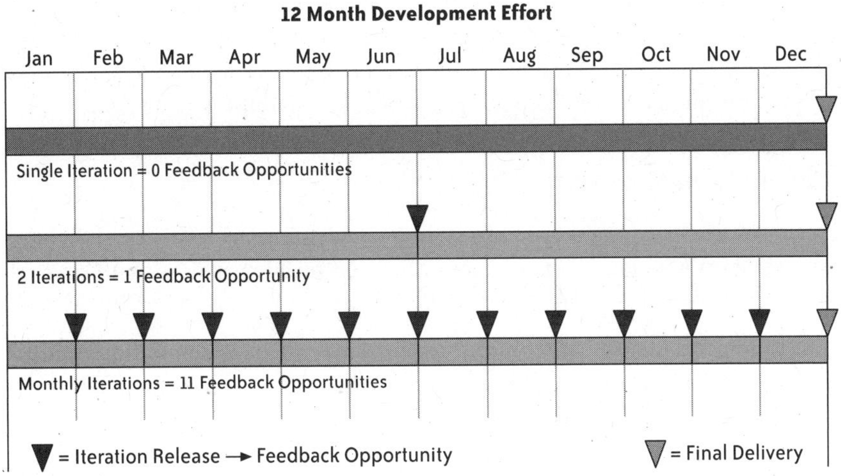

12 Month Development Effort

| Jan | Feb | Mar | Apr | May | Jun | Jul | Aug | Sep | Oct | Nov | Dec |

Single Iteration = 0 Feedback Opportunities

2 Iterations = 1 Feedback Opportunity

Monthly Iterations = 11 Feedback Opportunities

▼ = Iteration Release → Feedback Opportunity   ▽ = Final Delivery

FIGURE 7-1. Short iterations increase feedback opportunities

Customer feedback benefits a development effort in several ways. First, assuming we have learned our lesson about prioritized requirements by now, feedback allows developers to focus on the features most important to the customer. Each iteration implements a subset of the requirements, starting with the most important. Following each iteration, the requirements list is modified based on customer feedback; requirements are added, deleted, modified, and reprioritized. The next iteration again implements a subset of the updated requirements in priority order, so developers are always implementing the requirements most important to the customer, even if the priorities are completely different from the previous iteration.

The cycle just described has a couple of important side effects: requirements changes are accounted for automatically, and domain knowledge gained in early iterations can be applied to subsequent iterations, making those iterations more efficient.

Frequent feedback limits over-investing in one area of the project by giving the customer an opportunity to indicate a feature is "good enough." Although further refinement of the feature may be possible and may improve the final product, continued refinement past a certain point generates diminishing returns. The additional time spent on "good enough" features may be better spent in areas where the return is greater.

Finally, feedback ensures that the right product is built. Initial requirements are often generated without a good understanding of what's really needed. By providing many interim releases via short iterations, developers allow customers to gain a better understanding of the requirements and to see the realm of possibilities. Customer feedback at regular intervals allows developers to change the direction of development, drop or add features, or stop development in areas with diminishing returns.

Feedback also has a positive effect on the developer-to-customer relationship. A customer who provides feedback and sees that feedback reflected in the next iteration will feel a part of the process. In addition to fostering goodwill between the customer and the development team, this feeling will encourage the customer to spend more time evaluating the product and providing better feedback, since he knows it will be taken seriously.

Make Course Corrections

Getting feedback from customers is half the job. Implementing the feedback in the product is the other half. Short iterations allow frequent course corrections, which can be used to home in on the target.

Two types of problems that can arise during development are miscommunication between customers and developers, and changing requirements. You can address both problems by making course corrections based on customer feedback.

Miscommunication between customers and developers manifests itself as features in the product that don't behave the way the customer intended. For example, a word processor document may have the following user story, a form of requirement described in Mike Cohn's book, *User Stories Applied* (Addison-Wesley Professional, 2004):

> As an author, I want to make a copy of the current document so I can save a snapshot before continuing to write.

The story doesn't specify what to name the copy, so developers might assume that the name should be in the typical *Copy (x) of myfile.doc* format and implement it this way. At the end of the iteration, the application is shown to the customer, who immediately points out that the copy's name should be formatted as *myfile(x).doc*. As shown in Figure 7-2, developers respond to this feedback by adding a note to the user story to bring it in line with the customer's needs and changing the implementation in the next iteration.

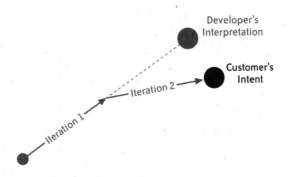

FIGURE 7-2. Course correction due to initial miscommunication

Requirements change when the customer determines that the original requirements no longer reflect the required functionality. Such changes may occur for any number of reasons, but the result is an implementation that is no longer in line with the customer's requirements. Perhaps the customer has decided to switch from a client-server application to a web services application running in a browser. In this case, the developers are given a new direction and must make a major course correction, as in Figure 7-3.

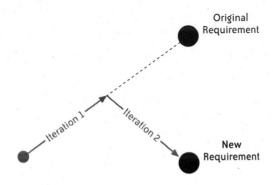

FIGURE 7-3. Course correction due to changing requirements

The ability to make course corrections depends on getting feedback from the customer; the ability to make course corrections quickly and efficiently depends on short iterations, which generate the necessary feedback in a timely fashion.

Developing with Short Iterations

The techniques that support short iterations are straightforward. The first two—prioritized requirements and a fixed iteration length—work together to ensure that developers are always working toward getting the customer's highest priority requirements implemented. The remaining techniques—demonstrating the iteration's product and delivering functional software to the customer—help focus the team on meeting its goals of providing value and getting useful feedback.

Work to Prioritized Requirements

Prioritized requirements can help minimize the size of the codebase (see Chapter 6), but they play a role in short iterations as well. Focusing on the most important requirements delivers the most useful functionality to the customer, so short iterations that implement the most important features first deliver the most value in the shortest time.

Set an Iteration Length and Stick to It

Although most Agile methodologies recommend iteration lengths of two to six weeks, several factors influence iteration length, including the volatility of the environment, experience with the methodology in use, the technical ability of the team and its understanding of the technologies in use, and the complexity of the system itself.

Choosing an iteration length within the two- to six-week range, or in some cases outside of it, will depend on each of those factors. However, unless dictated otherwise by experience or knowledgeable recommendation, the best starting point is in the middle of that range—four weeks.

The customer's understanding of the domain, the level of competition within the domain, and the volatility of the domain itself all combine to drive the volatility of the environment. You will typically find a lower rate of change when developing for a customer who is the major force in a domain and has very little competition than you will when developing for a startup company in a brand new field with many players. Development within a research organization may be quite a bit more hectic, as new technologies, or uses for them, drive frequent requirements changes.

Team experience can also affect iteration length. A team with lots of experience using the development process will be more efficient than a less experienced one, and will be able to get more done in a shorter iteration. The same holds true for the team's experience with the technologies being used. The need to research a technology before using it in a product can slow the pace of development significantly.

Finally, the complexity of the system can affect the pace of development. Systems with many external components place an integration burden on the team, and systems requiring lots of infrastructure development can generate tasks that span multiple iterations.

Regardless of the iteration length chosen, adherence to that length is very important, so set an end date for each iteration up front. Make sure everyone (especially management) understands that the date is not negotiable and that if development begins to get behind schedule, you will omit functionality in order to make the release date. An inviolable end date does two things: it ensures that the customer gets new functionality to evaluate regularly, and it focuses the development team.

Customer feedback is one of the main drivers for short iterations; without new functionality to evaluate, customers can't provide useful feedback. If a development team allows the end dates to slip, or even worse, allows date slippage to become a habit, the ability to get and incorporate feedback will be at risk. Better to get feedback on less functionality than on none at all.

Iteration end dates also focus the team on the task at hand. A team that knows when it has to deliver tends to stay focused on the requirements, especially when the iteration always ends with a demonstration in front of the customer.

End Each Iteration with a Demo

An end-of-iteration demonstration serves two purposes: it recognizes the development team's effort, and it officially marks the end of the iteration.

Ending the iteration with a demo gives the development team a chance to show off what it has been doing over the course of the iteration. A positive reaction from the customer provides a sense of accomplishment and builds enthusiasm for the next iteration. An end-of-iteration demo also focuses the team on the work it's doing. No one wants to stand up in front of the customer and announce that no new functionality is ready, so the entire team has a vested interest in implementing requirements and avoiding tasks that do not help reach that goal. It also drives home the point that delivering new functionality is important, enough so that finishing a few of the requirements is better than half-finishing all the requirements.

An end-of-iteration demo is the team's declaration that it has completed the work it agreed to for the iteration and signifies the official handoff to the customer. It indicates to the customer that the team is dedicated to reaching milestones and delivering on promises. Both the team and the customer are afforded a sense of completion that punctuates the team's progress.

Deliver the Iteration's Product to the Customer

While the end-of-iteration demo introduces customers to the iteration's product, it isn't enough to generate good feedback. Customers need time to dig into the product and apply it to the tasks for which it will eventually be used. Only after customers have had time to really put the product through its paces will they begin to provide useful feedback, so the product must be delivered to the end users.

Delivering the product doesn't necessarily mean shipping the product in fancy packaging; it can be as simple as giving customers access to a distribution file on an FTP server. The means of delivery will depend on the type of product under development: client applications may be distributed via CD/DVD, web applications may be distributed by updating a server, software for phones or PDAs may require providing hardware with the new application loaded. Whatever the method, getting the software in the customer's hands so they can use it in their own environment is essential to getting good feedback.

The Fallacy of Iterative Development

Iterative development is an effective approach for creating software products. However, the desire to create deterministic plans and schedules sometimes leads to an implementation that marginalizes the benefits of iterative development. The *fallacy of iterative development* is the following pair of false assumptions about iterative development:

- Iterative development is a series of short Waterfalls.
- The content of all iterations should be defined at the outset by divvying up the requirements.

These assumptions lead to a process, shown in Figure 7-4, in which all requirements are gathered at the beginning of the development cycle and an upfront planning activity determines the content of all iterations by divvying up the requirements into iteration-sized pieces, typically with each iteration focused on a different area of the product. The product is then developed via a series of iterations, each of which has the typical Waterfall phases of design, implementation, and test (remember, we eliminated the integration phase with continuous integration). Although this approach is incremental (new features are added each iteration), it doesn't incorporate customer feedback by reevaluating requirements after each iteration. Features implemented during the iteration are considered complete, and the iteration that follows simply moves on to the next feature.

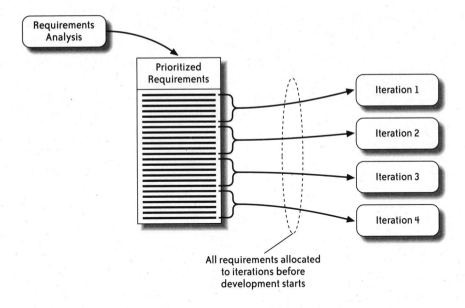

FIGURE 7-4. Requirements assigned during upfront planning

Two problems can arise from this type of iterative development: customer input is ignored, or the effort is replanned numerous times. Planning the entire development effort at the outset doesn't leave room for change based on customer feedback. The development team forges ahead based on the plan, even in the face of customer feedback indicating it is headed in the wrong direction. The end result of sticking to the original plan and ignoring customer feedback is that the development team builds the wrong product.

Incorporating customer feedback after each iteration is important, but when that feedback is incorporated through replanning of the remaining iterations, the result is a lot of wasted effort. For a 12-month development effort using 1-month iterations, 12 iterations are planned at the beginning of the effort. Following the first iteration, the remaining 11 iterations are replanned based on customer feedback. After the second iteration, the remaining 10 iterations are replanned, and so on until the end of the effort. Although customer feedback is being incorporated, much of the planning effort is wasted. The final iteration is planned 12 times, but only the last plan is executed.

The solution to both problems is to plan only the next (short) iteration in detail, as shown in Figure 7-5. Customer needs are captured by the prioritized requirements list, so the list is updated at the start of each iteration. Planning for each iteration is simply a matter of selecting a subset of the requirements from the top of the list.

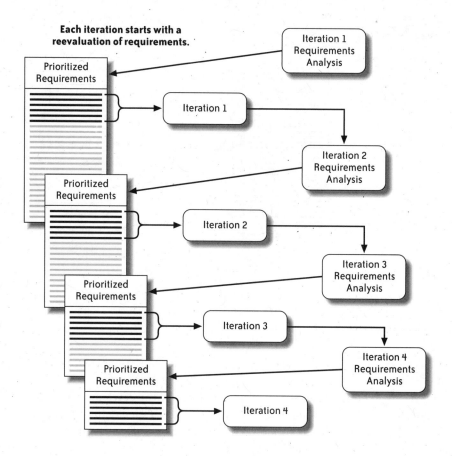

FIGURE 7-5. Requirements reassessed at the start of each iteration

Planning short iterations one at a time from an updated requirements list guarantees that the development team is always working the issues that are most important to the customer and that the final product is what the customer needs. In addition, no effort is wasted trying to plan too far ahead.

Big Tasks in Little Pieces

The single biggest objection to developing in short iterations is that some tasks are just too big to fit. System architecture is often placed in this category, as is the development of complex functionality that "doesn't work unless all the pieces are there." On the surface, these may seem like valid arguments, and in traditional Waterfall development, they are. However, changing the development paradigm addresses both arguments.

Emergent design allows the component-level architecture to evolve as requirements become more defined. When evolving an architecture over time, short iterations actually aid development. The quick turnaround times resulting from short iterations provide timely feedback on what works, allow architects to try multiple approaches, and postpone critical decisions until the system is better understood.

Emergent design doesn't relieve system architects of all need to think ahead. For example, attempting to retrofit security onto an existing system can result in lots of redesign and rewriting. However, adequate consideration of security issues early on doesn't require implementing a full-blown security component in the first iteration.

The implementation of complex functionality often doesn't fit in one iteration, which can mean that the development team has no functional software to release at the end of the demo. However, complex functionality can typically be broken into smaller, less complex pieces. Simulating nonexistent components or incomplete functionality through the use of mock objects and method stubs allows development to proceed without all the pieces in place. As development proceeds, components and functionality are integrated incrementally until the mock objects and stubs are eventually replaced with the real thing. This approach allows the team to demonstrate functional software following each iteration.

Summary

Short iterations deliver functional software to the customer regularly and frequently, allowing customer feedback to play an integral role in the ongoing development process.

Short iterations support Lean software development principles such as eliminating waste, deferring commitment until the last reasonable moment, and delivering functional software quickly.

Short iterations are driven by the need to increase customer feedback and make course corrections throughout the development cycle, both of which help ensure that the final product is what the customer really needs.

Working to a prioritized requirements list is one of the enabling techniques for implementing short iterations. Prioritized lists ensure that the team is working on the most important features.

Strictly enforcing a standard iteration length and presenting the iteration output to the customer help keep the development team focused on the requirements scheduled for the current iteration.

Delivering the iteration output to the customer, or at least making it available for testing and experimentation, gives the customer time to determine which features fit their needs and which need more work or should be dropped. More evaluation time generates better feedback and, ultimately, a better product.

CHAPTER EIGHT

Practice 5: Customer Participation

Doing a great job and not meeting the customer's objectives is as useless as doing a poor job within
the customer's objectives.

—Thomas Faranda

If the goal of product development is to create a product the customer will use, it stands to reason that customer participation is an integral part of the process. Although customer participation is listed as the fifth practice, its importance should not be underestimated. The concepts of prioritized requirements and course corrections based on customer feedback both require active customer participation.

Customers are the best source of information about the problem domain. They know the tasks that have to be done, they know the conditions in which the solution must perform, and they know the goals they are trying to achieve with the solution. They seldom know much about the technologies used to implement the solution.

Developers, on the other hand, do know the technologies. They know the features of the latest languages and development environments, they understand the tradeoffs between different technologies, and they know the most efficient ways to model problems and solutions. What they don't know are the intricacies of the domain—the business knowledge the solution must incorporate.

Combining the business knowledge of the customer with the technical savvy of the development team creates a team dynamic that drives better solutions. Customers provide objectives to developers and developers show customers the art of the possible, which in turn allows customers to imagine new possibilities. Developers and customers inspire each other to create something better than either can individually.

Customer Participation Is a Two-Way Street

Development teams need customer input in the form of requirements and priorities, but they must also keep the customer informed about the work in progress. Customers need to be forthcoming with feedback, and development teams must act on that feedback. Involving the customer in all aspects of the development process is the best way to create the required two-way information flow.

Involve the Customer Throughout the Development Process

Traditional customer participation consists of input during the requirements analysis phase and the generation of change requests following delivery of the final product. Lean software development strives for a much higher level of customer participation. Customers not only participate in the development of requirements, but they also actually write and prioritize the requirements and define the acceptance tests used to decide when requirements have been satisfied. Throughout the development cycle, customers are available to resolve ambiguities and answer questions for developers. With a continuous integration system that includes autodeployment, customers can check the progress of the team and run user tests to ensure that requirements are being met.

Keep the Customer Informed

Involving customers in the development process means keeping them informed of what's going on. Customers should be informed of the goals of each iteration as well as the team's progress toward those goals. Customers should also be informed of any problems that arise during the development effort. An upfront approach to reporting problems increases the trust between the development team and the customer, and it gives the customer a chance to take action (such as reprioritizing requirements) to mitigate delays caused by such problems.

Providing access to the product during the iteration can be an effective way to keep the customer informed. Using the application, even in a primitive state, lets customers see what's really being developed. It allows them to watch their feedback being incorporated into the product, which builds customer confidence in the development team.

Act on Customer Feedback

Acting on the customer's feedback is the key to maintaining customer involvement throughout the development effort. A customer who feels his input is being heard and put to use is more likely to continue providing that input.

Customer feedback generated through using the iteration's output can be useful in generating new requirements, modifying or deleting existing requirements, and reprioritizing requirements; however, feedback can be useful at any point during the development cycle. For example, customers who monitor progress via an autodeployed version of the product can provide guidance on requirements currently under development.

Paving the Street

Every development effort is unique. Different customers have different ways of interacting with the development team, and different products require different types of interactions. The following techniques are by no means exhaustive, but they provide a starting point for developing a collaborative relationship between the customer and the team.

Designate a Product Owner

Each product should have a champion, typically called a product owner, whose job is representing the customer's needs during the development cycle. The product owner is the voice of the customer, and it is his job to define value from the customer's point of view for the development team. A product owner often is responsible for maintaining the prioritized requirements and acts as a common point of contact for the development team and the customer.

Some development teams are lucky enough to have a full-time, on-site customer to fill the product owner role. However, most teams will have only periodic contact with customers, or, in the case of mass-produced products, the customer will not be a single entity but rather a disparate collection of users. Whether on-site customers or proxies, product owners must understand the needs of the customer and the business domain of the solution being developed. Furthermore, product owners must avoid conflicts of interest when championing the customer's point of view, so they should not be members of the development team.

Engage the Customer in Writing Requirements and Acceptance Tests

Engaging customers in writing requirements and tests helps eliminate confusion and misinterpretations when the development team begins to implement requirements. Instead of providing developers with a problem description to be decomposed into requirements, customers describe the features they want and the criteria for determining completion. Having customers write requirements and tests also gives customers a feeling that they are involved in the process, and it goes a long way toward keeping them informed of what the development team is working on.

Requirements define what to implement, and acceptance tests demonstrate that the requirement has been met. The closer these two things align with the customer's needs, the more successful the product will be in solving the customer's problem, and the best way to align them is to have the customer create them.

To help engage customers, provide a specific mechanism for them to supply their input. Giving the customer direct access to a requirements and test repository is an easy approach, particularly if access is via a web application. However, direct access may not be feasible for several reasons, including security issues, large numbers of customers, or customer understanding of the process.

Another approach is face-to-face contact with the customer on a regular basis. Developing requirements through face-to-face brainstorming and prioritizing allows customers to present their requirements and gives the development team a chance to clarify vague requirements firsthand.

Provide Project Status

One aspect of keeping the customer informed is reporting the project status. Items of interest to the customer include:

- Content of the current iteration
- Work completed or remaining in the iteration
- Test results
- Issues affecting completion of the iteration

One way to provide the access is through a "dashboard" application. Easily accessed by customers, management, and the development team, dashboards ensure that everyone gets the same, up-to-date view of the project status. Dashboards can include such things as requirements selected for implementation during an iteration, burndown charts that track the amount of work remaining in an iteration, and test results indicating which requirements have passed the customer's acceptance tests and are considered complete. A number of Lean and Agile software life cycle management tools exist, and most include a dashboard application, which is typically a web application providing easy access for all the project's stakeholders.

Although dashboards can convey project status, they don't always provide an adequate forum for reporting specific problems to the customer. A more detailed explanation, as well as the discussion of potential solutions, requires a more flexible approach. One such approach is a wiki, which provides a free-form forum and allows everyone to post comments and pertinent information.

Lean software development teams often make use of daily standup meetings where team members discuss their progress and present problems with which they need assistance. Allowing customers to listen in on daily meetings is another way to provide detailed project status.

Provide Access to the Product

In Chapter 7, we pointed out the need to deliver each iteration's product to the customer. Here we are addressing a slightly different need. By having access during the iteration, the customer can see the work progress. Instead of waiting until the end of the iteration to see how a particular feature is being implemented, customers can see the feature take shape and provide immediate feedback.

The form of product access depends on the nature of the product. For example, web applications can be pushed to test servers accessible by the customer, client applications can make use of automatic updates, and standalone applications can be wrapped up in installation kits or compressed archives. Adding an autodeployment task to a continuous integration implementation ensures that the latest build is always functional (even when incomplete) and available to the customer, regardless of the distribution method.

Create a Feedback Path

An easy-to-use feedback mechanism is essential for gathering customer input. Any mechanism requiring too much effort won't be used, and the quality of feedback will suffer. The developers' end of the feedback path must be easy-to-use as well, since even the best feedback is useless if it never reaches the developers. Three feedback approaches that are available to development teams are form-based reporting, interactive applications, and face-to-face meetings.

Form-based feedback, such as email and forms on web pages, is a good approach to use with large, independent customers. Although customers may feel less connected than with other approaches, form-based feedback allows a much higher volume since developers are not required to interact with every customer. It also lends itself well to tracking individual problems, since each form submittal can be numbered and recorded.

Interactive applications are typically web applications, which allow easy access via web browsers and avoid the need for customers to load client software. Examples of interactive online applications include wikis, blogs, and chat rooms. Each of these approaches allows customers to interact directly with developers, lending immediacy to the feedback loop. Interactive solutions are effective when the number of customers is small and they are not colocated with the developers.

Face-to-face meetings are the ultimate in flexible one-on-one interactions and allow customers and developers to work closely together to resolve issues and clarify ambiguities. However, to be an efficient feedback mechanism, meetings have to be held on a regular basis; short, frequent meetings similar to the development team's daily standups are best. This approach can prove difficult with customers who are not colocated, and it can be impossible with a large customer base, so face-to-face meetings are best for dedicated customers with on-site representatives.

Find CRACK Customer Representatives

Customer participation relies on having dedicated and, if possible, colocated customer representatives. In their 2003 book *Balancing Agility and Discipline* (Addison-Wesley Professional), Barry Boehm and Richard Turner discuss the need for CRACK customer representatives, meaning representatives who are:

Collaborative
    They work well with the development team.

Representative
    They understand the point of view of the end user.

Authorized
    They are empowered to make decisions.

Committed
    They share the development team's dedication to creating a good product.

Knowledgeable
    They have the understanding and experience necessary to provide guidance.

CRACK customer representatives provide immediate access to the customer's thinking on requirements and acceptance tests. They clarify requirements for developers, validate acceptance tests, and help keep developers focused on customer needs. Furthermore, customer representatives can form part of the status mechanism that keeps the customer informed and part of the feedback loop that provides customer input to the development team.

Customer representatives often function as product owners, where their intimate knowledge of the customer's needs allows them to manage the requirements driving development.

An All-Too-Common Problem

Although the ideal is to have CRACK customer representatives on site, they often are not available throughout the development effort. Perhaps the customer can't afford to dedicate someone full-time to the project, or the customer consists of individual users. In cases like these, customer proxies can take the place of customer representatives.

Customer proxies should embody the same CRACK characteristics as customer representatives, but they also need to be willing to stand up to the development team and even management on behalf of the customer. Often, someone who has used the customer's products in the past or has experience working in the same business domain as the customer can be an effective customer proxy. Although he may not be as familiar with a specific customer's thinking, he must at least be knowledgeable about the problem domain.

Earlier we pointed out that product owners shouldn't be members of the development team due to the potential for conflicts of interest. Because customer proxies often serve as product owners and champion the customer's point of view, they should not be members of the development team either.

Summary

Customers understand the business domain. Developers understand the technologies. Combining customer knowledge with development technical know-how is a recipe for success.

Customer/developer collaboration requires bidirectional flow of information between customers and developers, and it requires both parties to participate actively in the collaboration. Developers must provide status and act on feedback; customers must provide prioritized requirements, evaluate the product, and provide useful feedback.

Give customers an active role in the development of the product by designating product owners and engaging customers in writing requirements and acceptance tests.

Keep customers informed and involved by providing project status, access to the product throughout development, and an easy-to-use feedback mechanism.

A knowledgeable, involved customer representative, whether a CRACK representative or a customer proxy, is invaluable in creating and delivering a product that meets the customer's needs.

CHAPTER NINE

What Next?

It is impossible for a man to learn what he thinks he already knows.

—Epictetus

Fully implementing the core practices laid out in the last five chapters takes time. If you have implemented some or all of these practices, you have already seen significant increases in both productivity and quality. This means that you no longer need to be convinced; rather, you are excited about the possibilities and anxious to learn what to do next.

Lean Thinking and the Analysis Practices

Lean is a way of thinking, a certain perspective on improving productivity and quality. This mindset cuts across all areas to which Lean has been applied (or will be applied). The more you read about how Lean thinking has been applied in other areas of business, the more you will come to understand how to apply these techniques to your own situation in software development.

Overall, the Lean software development practices can be roughly divided into two categories: the concrete practices and the analysis practices. Up to this point we have been presenting the core concrete practices. In this chapter we introduce you to some of the analysis practices that will help you identify the remaining bottlenecks and how to further improve your software development process.

You *could* start your Lean software development journey with the analysis practices. The problem is that this would require you to more fully understand the Lean perspective and principles at the outset. In the end, if done correctly, it would probably lead you (at first) to the very same concrete practices. We think it's better just to start with the concrete practices and learn as you go.

Although the concrete practices will definitely bring significant quality and productivity improvements, that is just the tip of the iceberg. The analysis practices have the potential for even greater productivity and quality gains, especially when they take into account the larger business processes in which the software development occurs. Implementing the concrete practices will give you the experience and knowledge you need to effectively use the analysis practices.

It can be very beneficial to read some of the classic books on Lean manufacturing and some related areas. This will help you to think from a Lean perspective. Some of our recommended reading would include *Lean Thinking* by James Womack et al. (Free Press, 2003), *The Toyota Way* by Jeffrey Liker (McGraw-Hill, 2003), *The Toyota Product Development System* by James Morgan and Jeffrey Liker (Productivity Press, 2006), and *The Goal* by Eliyahu Goldratt and Jeff Cox (North River Press, 2004).

The remainder of this chapter will describe some of the Lean analysis practices as well as some closely related practices from other business management strategies, such as Six Sigma and the Theory of Constraints. Lean isn't above adopting practices from other areas. As such, Agile methodologies, Six Sigma, and ToC would all be considered valid Lean practices if they result in delivering more value to the customer more quickly.

Probably the most well-known Lean analysis practice is *value stream mapping* (VSM). We cover VSM as well as a number of other analysis practices, such as Kaizen Workshops, root cause analysis, and some practices that straddle the gray area between concrete and analytical.

In this chapter we discuss:

- Kaizen
- Kaizen Workshops
- Value stream mapping
- Root cause analysis
- Kanban
- Other complementary approaches

Kaizen

In Japanese, Kaizen means "continuous improvement." It is derived from the Japanese words *kai* (meaning "change") and *zen* (meaning "good").

Kaizen is therefore a system of slow, continuous, incremental improvements. As such, it involves every employee, from top management to the clerk. Everyone is encouraged, even expected, to come up with small suggestions for improvements on a regular basis. Typically, a supervisor will review an improvement suggestion within 24 hours, and if approved, it will be quickly implemented.

Toyota, for example, has been practicing company-wide Kaizen for over 50 years, and it still implements tens of thousands of improvements each year. At Canon, Inc., supervisors are required to set aside 30 minutes each day for workers to identify problems and suggest solutions. Other meetings are not to be held during "Kaizen Time," and supervisors are not even supposed to answer the phone.

This is a cultural system that must be actively supported by top management. It is literally the opposite of the "if it isn't broke, don't fix it" mentality, being more of an "improve it even if it isn't broken, because if we don't, we can't compete with those that do" mentality.

Driving the cultural changes required to bring Kaizen to an entire company is only possible with strong and consistent support from the very top. It is not possible for an individual manager or engineer involved in software development to do this alone. But you can bring it to your team, project, or department, and the Kaizen basics are quite simple:

- Standardize a process
- Measure the performance of that process
- Implement a change and measure its effect on performance

- Change the standard to include the improvement
- Repeat the cycle forever

The key to making this work is to institutionalize the whole process in some way (as Canon did) so that there really is a steady stream of small improvements (not just one or two a year). The number of suggested improvements by a worker should be an important part of the assessment of his supervisor's performance. Management must work hard to consider and implement suggestions, and workers need to be recognized for their contributions.

Kaizen requires a deep cultural commitment and can be difficult to sustain, but it is worth striving for. (As Toyota has demonstrated, it creates a long-term competitive advantage.) However, when you are new to Lean and you've just finished implementing the concrete practices, it would be better to begin your first foray into the analysis practices with *Kaizen Workshops*.

Kaizen Workshops

When the term Kaizen is used in the West, people are usually talking about a Kaizen Workshop and not the Kaizen system described in the previous section. The Kaizen Workshop has been used under several other names: Kaizen Blitz, Kaizen Event, Accelerated Improvement Workshop, Rapid Process Improvement Workshop, and even simply Workouts. In this chapter, we will use the term Kaizen Workshop.

A Kaizen Workshop is an intense, focused project to improve a process, where a team or department throws all of its resources into the effort for a short period of time. The intensity and urgency is designed to overcome any institutionalized resistance. The execution is swift, and it is expected that there will be significant results very quickly.

There are two fundamental principles behind a Kaizen Workshop:

- Don't just plan...act!
- It's better to get a 50% improvement now than to wait months hoping for perfection.

First, you must identify a specific problem that you want to address. Then you can hold a Kaizen Workshop to find and implement solutions.

A Kaizen Workshop is a structured rapid improvement process that has three phases:

- Plan (4 to 6 weeks)
- Workshop (3 to 5 days)
- Implement (1 to 3 months)

A Kaizen Workshop requires considerable planning because it must bring together all stakeholders into an integrated team. All required information and material must be gathered before the workshop, and the relevant leadership must empower the workshop team to implement the resulting changes.

During the planning phase you assess your current situation and define the problem you want to address. Your major activities revolve around getting leadership commitment, lining up stakeholders to participate, and creating a formal charter for the Kaizen Workshop that everyone can agree to.

The Kaizen Workshop charter will define the problem to be addressed, the desired outcome, and the boundaries or scope of the resulting solution(s). It is vital that the leadership for the affected areas formally sign on to support the effort. They must commit to quickly accept or reject the recommendations of the Kaizen Workshop and to work to remove any roadblocks.

During the planning phase you hold meetings with the organization's leaders to get their perspective, instill the need to address the problem, and secure their commitment to support the Kaizen Workshop. This is also the time when you identify the workshop participants, including the stakeholders, experts, workers, and even customers, and get their commitment to support the Kaizen Workshop.

The workshop itself is a dedicated multiday affair, where all of the participants gather for uninterrupted time to come up with solutions. You start off with some basic training for all participants to make sure everyone understands how the workshop will operate and proceed. Then you typically review the current situation, the problem to be addressed, and the previously agreed-upon boundaries for the solutions. This is followed by brainstorming sessions and in-depth discussions..You will typically concentrate on things like quality (reducing defects), achieving flow, reducing cycle time, costs, or other wastes.

The goal is to have the workshop participants reach a consensus on one or more recommended action plans. These recommendations are sent to the Kaizen Workshop's leadership team, which has previously committed to rapid approval or rejection (usually within one day).

Finally, the Kaizen Workshop participants rapidly implement the approved recommendations, with the support of the leadership, taking no more than three months (preferably less). Monthly progress reports are made to the leadership team to ensure timely implementation and full accountability.

Value Stream Maps

Value stream mapping is a classic Lean analysis tool. If you've heard of Lean, chances are you've also heard of value stream mapping. It is one of the most powerful Lean tools and can be applied to almost any process.

A VSM is a visual representation of all the steps in a particular process from start to finish (usually from customer request through the resulting delivery to the customer). Attached to each step is data about that step, particularly the touch time (actual work time) and wait time. Each step is also identified as value-added, non-value-added, or non-value-added but necessary.

The VSM makes it easier to spot waste and bottlenecks in the process. Because it shows the entire product flow from end to end, you can also spot problems that originate outside of the core software development activities.

After the VSM has been created, some problems may become apparent. Any non-value-added steps, for example, would be pure waste and should be considered for elimination. Points in the value stream with large wait times or queues of work in progress are red flags that should invite closer scrutiny.

It is very important that the VSM show the process as it is actually carried out; do not bring your written process documents to the VSM exercise because we guarantee that the documented process is *not* the same as what you are actually doing. This helps make the tacit knowledge of the team explicit, and it can also point to areas where the documented process needs to be updated to reflect reality.

You may have noticed that a VSM focuses on time and not cost. A key insight of Lean thinking is that the best way to reduce cost is not to focus on cost at all, but to let cost get reduced as a byproduct of focusing on the root causes of increased cost: cycle time and quality.

Let's look at an example for a team maintaining an application. This team receives feature requests for its existing application that it then implements and deploys to the customer. Figure 9-1 shows a simplified VSM for this team's process. A more detailed VSM would break out more of the details in each processing box.

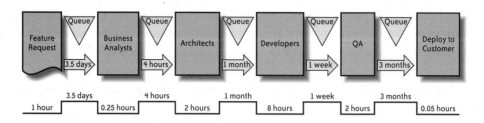

FIGURE 9-1. Simplified VSM

You can see that this team follows a fairly standard Waterfall process. In this case there is a queue between each process step. For VSMs in general, this is probably unusual, but it is very typical for a Waterfall software development process.

This team typically receives 18 feature requests each month, which then go through the following process:

1. Once a week, a business analyst rejects or approves (and prioritizes) all of the feature requests received in the previous week.

2. Architects estimate the implementation time and create a design for the feature.

3. Developers code and test the feature.

4. QA verifies that the feature works and satisfies the original requirement (feature request).

5. Every six months the company deploys a new release of its application containing all of the features implemented in the previous six months.

The VSM has been populated with time data based on its historical record. The timeline running along the bottom shows the value-added time in its lower segments and the wait time (or non-value-added time) in its upper segments. Even with this simplified VSM, a lot of things can be learned.

First off, how long does it take to implement and deploy a typical feature request? Adding the times in the timeline tells us that it takes about four months and five days. Looking at the bottom row of the timeline tells us that only 13.3 hours of that time is value-added. The vast majority of the time, features are waiting in a queue.

It's pretty obvious that one of the easiest ways this team could deliver value to the customer more quickly would be drastically reduce the time between deployments. The practice of having the company's business analysts triage the new features only once a week seems like an insignificant delay when the application is only deployed every six months. But if the deploy time is drastically reduced, the triage time will start to look significant, and it might start to make sense to handle feature requests in real time as they arrive.

A more detailed VSM might show steps that are completely non-value-added. Such steps, once identified, can be quickly eliminated.

Many VSMs will also show the typical number of work items in a queue, known as work in progress (WIP). They might also show the percent of work items that left a process step without defects (first-time quality). When analyzing a VSM, the primary goal is to find opportunities to reduce cycle time, minimize WIP, and maximize first-time quality.

Once improvement opportunities have been identified in a VSM, the next step is to draw a new VSM that incorporates the improvements. This is called the Future State VSM. Finally, a plan will be created for transitioning from the current VSM to the future VSM.

Other Lean Techniques

There are many more Lean techniques and practices that are more focused than the Lean analysis practices we just covered. These techniques can be applied in specific circumstances or for particular purposes. We'll briefly mention a few of them here.

Root Cause Analysis (Five Whys)

The Lean response to resolving a problem is not to merely fix the surface problem, but to find the root cause of the problem and fix that. *Root cause analysis* techniques are used to do this. Root cause analysis is not unique to Lean, but it is a fundamental part of Lean thinking.

There are many ways to do root cause analysis, but one of the most common and easiest to remember is known as the "five whys." This simply means asking the question "Why?" at least five times. For example:

Why did the application crash?
   Answer: Because the database schema didn't match what the application thought it was.

Why did the database schema not match the application's expectation?
   Answer: Because a bad hard disk required us to restore that database from a backup, and the restored database was from the previous version of the application, with an older schema.

Why wasn't the database restored from a version with the new schema?
   Answer: We didn't have one.

Why didn't we have one?
   Answer: Because database backups are made nightly and the hard disk crashed after the application was deployed but before the database was backed up.

Why didn't we make a database backup as part of the application deployment?
   Answer: That's not part of our deployment checklist.

Without doing a root cause analysis, the team might have just fixed the database to have the correct schema. However, this would leave the team vulnerable to having this problem recur in the future. The root cause analysis identified the actual root cause of the problem, and it resulted in an update to the deployment checklist to include backing up the database, thus preventing this problem from recurring in the future.

The preceding example had a single root cause. In many cases there are multiple root causes, so you have to keep this in mind as you do your analysis (a fishbone diagram provides a good way to capture multiple root causes of a particular problem). Also, five is not always the correct number of "whys." Make sure you reach the root cause before you stop asking.

Some other root cause analysis techniques you might want to research include:

- Pareto analysis
- Ishikawa diagram (fishbone diagram)
- Fault tree analysis
- Cause mapping

Kanban

We've talked quite a bit about delivering incremental value by using short iterations. In some situations, it may be preferable to use a continuous pipeline strategy rather than fixed iterations. Once a product moves into a sustaining mode with an expected steady stream of change requests and bug reports, a continuous pipeline process might make sense. This is when you would use a kanban system.

Kanban is a simple yet very effective scheduling system for maximizing flow and minimizing work in progress. It derives from the Japanese words *kan* (meaning "card") and *ban* (meaning "signal").

In a manufacturing environment, the kanban can be a card, a colored golf ball, an empty bin, or anything that can be used to indicate that a product or part has been depleted. A kanban is, in essence, a signal that will trigger replenishment of that product or part.

In Lean manufacturing, kanban is a key tool in implementing a pull-based assembly line. When a finished product is removed from the end of the line (due to a customer order), it pulls a replacement product from final assembly by sending it a kanban (that kanban is returned with the replacement product). If final assembly runs out of a part, final assembly sends a kanban to manufacture more of that part. This process cascades up the value stream, effectively pulling products through based on customer demand.

Small amounts of inventory are necessary at various stages in the manufacturing process to even out the manufacturing flow. You can control this by increasing or decreasing the number of kanbans at each step. A common Lean strategy is to start with plenty of kanbans at each step (lots of inventory) and then slowly reduce the number of kanbans to see where problems emerge in the value stream. After fixing the problems, the process can be repeated by once again reducing the number of kanbans.

So, how can this be applied to software development?

In software development, you will typically see a kanban system implemented using colored sticky notes on a whiteboard. Suppose that we have a sustainment process that takes each request through the following steps: design, implementation, test, build, and deploy. The kanban board might look like Figure 9-2. You can use different colors of sticky notes to denote different types of work items (such as bug reports or feature requests).

In a Lean system, the ideal is single-piece flow with no buffers or queues. In this example's process, it would mean that each state (design, implement, test, etc.) would have a single work item that is being handled in parallel with all the others, and that each state's work item would be the same size and they would all finish simultaneously and pass their work items on to the next state. We all know the probability of that happening is near zero.

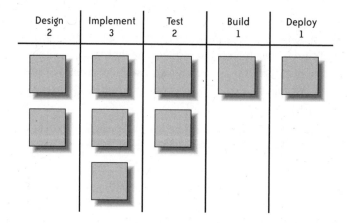

FIGURE 9-2. Kanban example

The problem with achieving the ideal is variation. The work items vary widely in size (some are small and some are large). In addition, the amount of time (for a given work item) in each state will also vary. For example, it usually (but not always) takes longer to implement a feature than is does to design it.

So, in our kanban example, each step has a WIP limit that is proportional to the amount of time that a typical work item is in that step. This limit is the maximum number of work items allowed to be in that state at any given instant. In this example, the implementation step has a limit of three, whereas the design and test steps have a limit of two. If a step is below its limit, it can grab a work item from the previous step as soon as it is available. If a step is at its limit, it must wait for one of its work items to complete *and* to be pulled into a downstream step before it can pull a work item from its upstream state.

This type of kanban board lets anyone on the team see the current state of affairs at a single glance.

Variations in the size of work items can still cause upstream steps to congest and downstream steps to temporarily starve. If this happens regularly, resources should be added or subtracted and the corresponding WIP limits adjusted to "balance the line."

However, sometimes all that is needed is to introduce a buffer to help even out the workflow. In Figure 9-3 we have added a queue that can hold one work item. This somewhat decouples the test step from the implementation step and ensures that the test step almost always has a work item immediately available (assuming the other limits are appropriately tuned).

In general, Lean would consider a queue to be a red flag for possible waste. However, when you consider its effect on the overall workflow, not having the queue might be even more wasteful. Small buffers, judiciously placed with the smallest feasible limits, can often improve the overall throughput. This would fall under the principle of optimizing the whole.

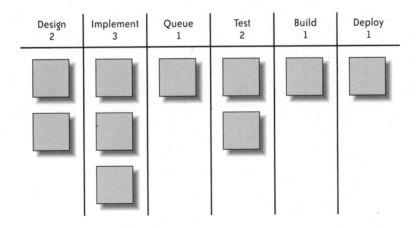

FIGURE 9-3. Kanban example with queue

Make It Visible

One common theme that you will find running through most Lean practices and implementations is the desire to make the state of the value stream immediately visible and obvious. Take any process (be it a manufacturing assembly line or a software development process) and devise a way to show, in real time, the overall status in a large, highly visible manner. The result is likely to be increased morale, productivity, and quality.

This happens because team members can now see the current status at a glance, giving them quick feedback on how the team is doing, and making it easy to spot problems before they get out of hand. This sense of control increases morale, satisfaction, and pride. In addition, management is better informed so that when problems do crop up, there is better cooperation between management and developers. Everyone works together toward a solution because everyone understands the situation in the same way.

The more you can do this, the more the benefits you will accrue. Let's briefly examine a few examples.

Kanban systems are a good example, as they almost always use some physical object to serve as a visible signal. An Internet search for "kanban software development" will turn up many pictures of kanban boards being used for software development. These pictures make it obvious that each of the kanban boards is communicating a lot of information at a glance.

A popular chart for showing the overall progress of a project is the burndown chart. Figure 9-4 shows a sample burndown chart. This chart shows the work remaining over time and can show at a glance whether the project is on track or not. Maintaining informative charts like this on a large whiteboard can provide the kind of visibility we've been talking about.

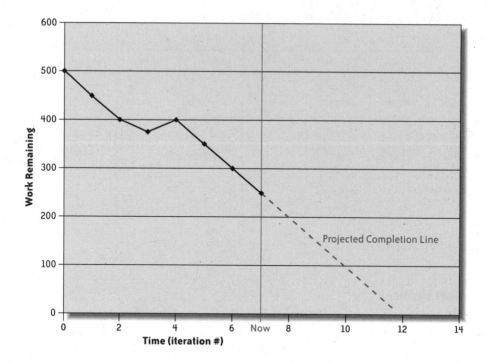

FIGURE 9-4. Burndown chart

If the team is not colocated, these kinds of charts have to be kept electronically. However, it's not good if people have to actually navigate somewhere to see the chart—this drastically reduces its usefulness. In this case, an equivalent method would give each location a large flat panel display that would hang in a highly visible location (above the coffee pots?) and always display the current chart(s) updated in real time.

A CI server is another good example of *making it visible*. A CI server monitors the source code repository for changes. When a change to the source code is detected, the CI server will retrieve a fresh copy of the source code, build the system, and run all automated tests. A CI server supports making it visible by bringing any failures in the automated build and test process to the immediate attention of the developers.

This could be as simple as displaying green or red on a web page. But that is not ideal because it requires someone to go and look. A better system would actively notify the developers (via email, RSS, SMS text message, etc.). We have heard of a very innovative approach that used a little bit of custom hardware that caused one of those old rotating, flashing red police lights to go off whenever the CI server found an error! This would be an example of an Andon display (mentioned in "Lean Speak" in Chapter 1).

Other Complementary Approaches

There are some complementary business management strategies whose methods and techniques are often combined with (or used by) Lean. As you read the literature on Lean, you'll run into these methods repeatedly. We won't discuss them in detail in this book, but we want to give you the basics so that you'll recognize them when you see them.

The ones you'll hear about most often are the *Theory of Constraints* (abbreviated as ToC), *Critical Chain* (ToC's engineering counterpart), *Six Sigma*, and *Capability Maturity Model Integration* (CMMI).

Theory of Constraints

ToC and Critical Chain (CC) are the brainchildren of Dr. Eliyahu Goldratt. They are based on a few simple principles and a set of problem-solving processes and tools for improving a business process (which includes the process of developing software). ToC and CC are based on the idea that at any given point in time there are one or more constraints limiting the performance of the overall process.

The tools and methods of ToC and CC are designed to help you identify these constraints and then remove them. This, of course, changes the system and results in new constraints. In the spirit of continuous improvement, this process of finding and removing constraints is applied repeatedly.

Once you start reading about ToC and CC, it is easy to see the parallels with Lean. There is currently a little bit of industry talk about applying ToC and CC to software development, but there are no serious efforts that we are aware of to actually do so.

Six Sigma

The goal in Six Sigma is to dramatically increase quality through root-cause defect reduction. The term "six sigma" comes from the mathematical field of statistics and refers to how far a process deviates from perfection. Six sigma specifically means no more than 3.4 defects per million opportunities—a very tough standard that requires near flawless execution. Six Sigma includes a number of tools and techniques (actually, an entire methodology) that are used to work toward this goal.

Although it is common to find Six Sigma combined with Lean in the manufacturing world, this is not the case in software development. An Internet search for "six sigma software development" will turn up a few references, but not much. Of late, Six Sigma has come under attack for stifling innovation. We suspect this will not encourage its adoption in the software world.

Capability Maturity Model Integration

CMMI is a process improvement approach that provides organizations with the essential elements of effective processes. It was originally developed for software development, but it has been adapted for use in other areas.

CMMI evaluates and measures the maturity of the software development process of an organization on a scale of 1 to 5, with 1 being the least mature and 5 being the most mature.

These are some of the characteristics of an immature organization:

- Process improvised during project
- Approved processes being ignored
- Reactive, not proactive
- Unrealistic budget and schedule
- Quality sacrificed for schedule
- No objective measure of quality

Contrast that with the characteristics of a mature organization:

- Intergroup communication and coordination
- Work accomplished according to plan
- Practices consistent with processes
- Processes updated as necessary
- Well-defined roles/responsibilities
- Management formally commits

CMMI provides industry best practices to support an organization's improvement work in a number of categories:

Process management
> These are practices for handling the overall process improvement cycle, including identifying needs, performing diagnoses, planning the improvements, and managing the deployment of improvements.

Project management
> These are best practices for planning and managing projects.

Engineering
> Technical best practices for performing the software or systems work.

Support
> These practices apply to support functions such as quality assurance and measurement.

If CMMI is implemented correctly in the intended spirit of genuine process improvement, it is very compatible with and complementary to the Lean approaches we have been espousing. The only thing to be wary of is the occasional organization that will implement a CMMI program as a "checklist" item solely to get a particular rating. This usually results in a heavy-handed process that is anything but Lean.

Where to Go from Here

We've finally arrived at the end of this book's journey, but we hope that it is just the beginning of your journey. Just remember the old quote that "Rome wasn't built in a day," and realize that change takes time, patience, and (most of all) perseverance.

We hope that we've provided you with a road map to help guide your initial foray into Lean software development. There is a substantial amount of detailed material that you can draw on for more specific advice about each topic that we have touched on here.

If you are going to be introducing Lean software development to your company or organization, you should be aware of one topic that we have not addressed: how to be an effective change agent.

That's a huge topic to which we could not even begin to do justice in this small book. So, we'll leave you with a couple of book recommendations that can help you learn the change agent skills you will need:

- *Fearless Change: Patterns for Introducing New Ideas* by Mary Lynn Manns and Linda Rising (Addison-Wesley, 2004)
- *Agile Adoption Patterns: A Roadmap to Organizational Success* by Amr Elssamadisy (Addison-Wesley Professional, 2008)

Remember, Lean is a journey, not a destination!

APPENDIX

Resources

As you read each chapter of this book, you may find yourself wanting to know more about a particular topic. In this appendix we have compiled a list of books and articles that we recommend as good starting points. We have grouped these recommendations by the chapters in this book to make it easy for you to find a relevant recommendation. Because of this organization, some recommendations may be repeated in more than one place.

Also, remember that there is a great deal of good, detailed information available on these topics for free on the Internet, so you don't always have to spend more money to learn more. Nevertheless, these books are among the best in their fields, so you won't go wrong reading any of them.

Chapter 1: Why Lean?

Larman, Craig. *Agile and Iterative Development: A Manager's Guide*. Boston, MA: Addison-Wesley Professional, 2003.

Liker, Jeffrey. *The Toyota Way*. New York, NY: McGraw-Hill, 2003.

Womack, James P., and Daniel T. Jones. *Lean Thinking: Banish Waste and Create Wealth in Your Corporation*, Second Edition. New York, NY: Free Press, 2003.

Chapter 2: Applying Lean to Software Development

Middleton, Peter, and James Sutton. *Lean Software Strategies: Proven Techniques for Managers and Developers*. New York, NY: Productivity Press, 2005.

Poppendieck, Mary, and Tom Poppendieck. *Implementing Lean Software Development: From Concept to Cash*. Boston: Addison-Wesley Professional, 2006.

Schwaber, Ken. *Agile Project Management with Scrum*. Seattle, WA: Microsoft Press, 2004.

Subramaniam, Venkat, and Andy Hunt. *Practices of an Agile Developer: Working in the Real World*. Raleigh, NC and Dallas, TX: Pragmatic Bookshelf, 2006.

Chapter 3: Practice 0: Source Code Management and Scripted Builds

Duvall, Paul, Steve Matyas, and Andrew Glover. *Continuous Integration: Improving Software Quality and Reducing Risk*. Boston, MA: Addison-Wesley Professional, 2007.

Mason, Mike. *Pragmatic Version Control: Using Subversion*, Second Edition. Raleigh, NC and Dallas, TX: Pragmatic Bookshelf, 2006.

Pilone, Dan, and Russ Miles. 2008. *Head First Software Development*. Sebastopol, CA: O'Reilly Media, Inc.

Chapter 4: Practice 1: Automated Testing

Feathers, Michael. *Working Effectively with Legacy Code*. Upper Saddle River, NJ: Prentice Hall PTR, 2004.

Koskela, Lasse. *Test Driven: Practical TDD and Acceptance TDD for Java Developers*. Greenwich, CT: Manning Publications, 2007.

Mugridge, Rick, and Ward Cunningham. *Fit for Developing Software: Framework for Integrated Tests*. Upper Saddle River, NJ: Prentice Hall PTR, 2005.

Chapter 5: Practice 2: Continuous Integration

Duvall, Paul, Steve Matyas, and Andrew Glover. *Continuous Integration: Improving Software Quality and Reducing Risk*. Boston, MA: Addison-Wesley Professional, 2007.

Chapter 6: Practice 3: Less Code

Ambler, Scott W., and Pramodkumar J. Sadalage. *Refactoring Databases: Evolutionary Database Design*. Boston, MA: Addison-Wesley Professional, 2004.

Bain, Scott L. *Emergent Design: The Evolutionary Nature of Professional Software Development*. Boston, MA: Addison-Wesley Professional, 2008.

Fowler, Martin, Kent Beck, John Brant, William Opdyke, and Don Roberts. *Refactoring: Improving the Design of Existing Code*. Boston, MA: Addison-Wesley Professional, 1999.

Kerievsky, Joshua. *Refactoring to Patterns*. Boston, MA: Addison-Wesley Professional, 2004.

Martin, Robert C. *Clean Code: A Handbook of Agile Software Craftsmanship*. Upper Saddle River, NJ: Prentice Hall PTR, 2008.

Poppendieck, Mary, and Tom Poppendieck. *Implementing Lean Software Development: From Concept to Cash*. Boston, MA: Addison-Wesley Professional, 2006.

Chapter 7: Practice 4: Short Iterations

Larman, Craig. *Agile and Iterative Development: A Manager's Guide*. Boston, MA: Addison-Wesley Professional, 2003.

Poppendieck, Mary, and Tom Poppendieck. *Implementing Lean Software Development: From Concept to Cash*. Boston, MA: Addison-Wesley Professional, 2006.

Schwaber, Ken. *Agile Project Management with Scrum*. Seattle, WA: Microsoft Press, 2004.

Chapter 8: Practice 5: Customer Participation

Cohn, Mike. *User Stories Applied: For Agile Software Development*. Boston, MA: Addison-Wesley Professional, 2004.

Poppendieck, Mary, and Tom Poppendieck. *Implementing Lean Software Development: From Concept to Cash*. Boston, MA: Addison-Wesley Professional, 2006.

Schwaber, Ken. *Agile Project Management with Scrum*. Seattle, WA: Microsoft Press, 2004.

Chapter 9: What Next?

Anderson, David J., and Eli Schragenheim. *Agile Management for Software Engineering: Applying the Theory of Constraints for Business Results*. Upper Saddle River, NJ: Prentice Hall PTR, 2003.

Boehm, Barry, and Richard Turner. *Balancing Agility and Discipline: A Guide for the Perplexed*. Boston, MA: Addison-Wesley Professional, 2003.

Elssamadisy, Amr. *Agile Adoption Patterns: A Roadmap to Organizational Success*. Boston, MA: Addison-Wesley Professional, 2008.

Manns, Mary Lynn, and Linda Rising. *Fearless Change: Patterns for Introducing New Ideas*. Boston, MA: Addison-Wesley, 2004.

Middleton, Peter, and James Sutton. *Lean Software Strategies: Proven Techniques for Managers and Developers*. New York, NY: Productivity Press, 2005.

Other

These are classic books that either don't fit in any of the earlier categories or span too many of these categories to fit into a single one. Still, they are such good, relevant books that we cannot bear to leave them out.

Brooks, Frederick P. *The Mythical Man-Month: Essays on Software Engineering, Anniversary Edition*, Second Edition. Boston, MA: Addison-Wesley Professional, 1995.

Goldratt, Eliyahu, and Jeff Cox. *The Goal: A Process of Ongoing Improvement*, Third Edition. Great Barrington, MA: North River Press, 2004.

Hunt, Andrew, and David Thomas. *The Pragmatic Programmer: From Journeyman to Master*. Boston, MA: Addison-Wesley Professional, 1999.

Morgan, James, and Jeffrey Liker. *The Toyota Product Development System: Integrating People, Process and Technology*. New York, NY: Productivity Press, 2006.

INDEX

A

acceptance tests
    engaging customers, 98
Agile Manifesto, 6
Agile methodologies, 8
Agile software development
    about, 5–9
    compared to Lean software development, 16,
        22
andon
    defined, 13
automated builds, 57–61, 58
automated testing, 38–53
    about, 38, 41
    approaches to, 49–53
    benefits of, 39
    resources about, 121
    types of, 43–49
autonomation
    about, 11

B

BDD (behavior-driven code)
    automated testing, 53
BDUF (Big Design Up Front)
    compared to YAGNI, 77
behavior tests
    about, 47
browser-based web applications
    user interface testing, 49
build scripts
    CI servers, 62
    creating, 68
    implementing, 63
build servers
    about, 61–62
    benefits of, 57
builds
    automated, 57–61, 58
    breaking, 30
    scripted, 120

burndown charts, 113

C

Capability Maturity Model Integration (CMMI),
    116
CC (Critical Chain), 115
centralized SCM systems, 29
changes
    handling in distributed SCM systems, 33
    handling in SCM systems, 30
    testing of, 39
CHAOS Report, 2
check-ins, 65
CI (continuous integration), 56–69
    about, 56
    build servers, 61
    end-to-end automated builds, 57–61
    hardware requirements, 67
    implementing, 63, 67–68
    quality, 65
    resources about, 121
    software, 57, 66
    software applications, 62
CI servers
    about, 62
    making state of the value stream visible, 114
    using, 64
classes
    testing, 43
CMMI (Capability Maturity Model Integration),
    116
Cockburn, Alistair
    on Lightweight methods, 6
codebases, 72
    (see also legacy code)
    developing less code, 75–81
    leaning out, 73
    resources, 121
    sharing under SCM, 34
    size of, 72
coding standards, 78
command-line SCM tools, 31

nonfunctional testing, 48
NUMMI automobile factory, 20

O

Ohno, Taiichi
    on the Toyota Production System, 10
optimizing
    whole processes, 22
organizations
    maturity of, 116
overproduction (type of waste), 12

P

partially completed work (type of waste), 19
    (see also inventory)
patterns (see design patterns)
people
    respect for, 22
perfection
    defined, 14
piggybacking
    on existing servers or shared computers, 67
Poppendieck, Mary and Tom
    on Lean software development, 16
practices, 25
    (see also idioms; principles; rules; standards;
    value statements)
    automated testing, 38–53
    CI (continuous integration), 56–69
    common to both Agile and Lean, 25
    customer participation, 96–101
    good coding, 74
    iterative development, 84–93
    less code, 72–81
    source code management and scripted builds,
        28–35
principles, 13
    (see also idioms; practices; rules; standards;
    value statements)
    Agile software development method, 7
    Kaizen, 105
    Lean software development, 13, 16–22
    for less code, 75
    for new code, 74
prioritization
    code requirements, 75
    iterative development, 88
    MoSCoW rules, 9
    of requirements, 75
    task size, 92
    tasks, 65
processes
    optimizing, 22
processing (type of waste), 12

product owners
    role of, 97
project status
    informing customers, 98
propagation
    of defects, 66
pull
    defined, 14

Q

quality, building in, 20
    CI, 65

R

red state, 51
refactor state, 52
refactoring
    codebases, 80
    design patterns, 79
    skills required for, 80
reporting
    build results from CI servers, 62
    results of end-to-end builds, 60
requirements, 98
    (see also specifications; executable
    specifications; standards)
    engaging customers, 98
    prioritizing, 76
resources about Lean development, 120–122
respect
    for people, 22
results
    build results for CI servers, 62
    end-to-end automated builds, 60
reusing
    code, 78
revision control (see SCM)
root cause analysis, 110
    (see also five whys)
Royce, Winston
    on the Waterfall method, 5
RSS feeds
    reporting end-to-end build results, 61
rules
    CI, 64
running
    automated tests, 42

S

scheduling
    CI builds, 63
SCM (source code management)
    about, 28–33
    resources about, 120

W

waiting (type of waste), 12
waste
    eliminating, 16
    types of, 11
waste in software development
    defects, 17
    delays, 19
    extra features, 17
    handoffs, 18
    partially completed work, 19
    task switching, 19
    unneeded processes, 20
Waterfall software development method, 4
    failure of, 5, 22, 108
web applications
    user interface testing, 49
web pages
    reporting end-to-end build results, 61
whys, five
    root cause analysis, 110
Workshops, Kaizen, 106
writing
    requirements and acceptance tests, 98

X

XP software development methodology, 9

Y

YAGNI (You Ain't Gonna Need It)
    codebases, 77

Z

zero-level practices, 28

About the Authors

Curt Hibbs has always been slightly obsessed with new technologies and tracking technology trends. But he will tell you that this is simply because he is lazy, always looking for new methods and technologies to make his work easier and more productive. This led to his discovery of Ruby in 2001 (when it was still relatively unknown outside of Japan) and to his founding several highly successful Ruby open source projects. For most of his professional career, which started in the 1970s, Curt has been a consultant to well-known companies such as Hewlett-Packard, Intuit, Corel, WordStar, Charles Schwab, Vivendi Universal, and more. He has also been a principal in several startups. Curt now works as a senior software engineer for The Boeing Company in St. Louis, Missouri.

Steve Jewett is a software developer with The Boeing Company, where he is involved in the development of network-centric cognitive decision support systems. His software experience started with BASIC and FORTRAN on a DEC PDP 1170 back in high school. The trail from there to the present day includes a litany of languages, a broad spectrum of design strategies and development methodologies, and a bevy of software projects, some of which were actually successful. Over a 20+ year career, he has developed software for automated test equipment, weapon/aircraft integration, embedded systems, desktop applications, and web applications. His primary areas of interest are software architecture design and software development methodologies, particularly Agile software development and its relationship to Lean processes.

Mike Sullivan has over six years of experience teaching at the university level, and he has spent the last four years working with software teams in small companies and large corporations to drive valuable solutions and improve team dynamics. He is currently working in a small research team within a large corporation, implementing Lean techniques to improve the software his team delivers. Mike's interests include golf, Cardinals baseball, and teaching.

Colophon

The cover image is a stock photograph from iStockphoto. The text font is Adobe's Meridien; the heading font is ITC Bailey.

The O'Reilly Advantage

Stay Current and Save Money

Order books online:
www.oreilly.com/store/order

Questions about our
products or your order:
order@oreilly.com

Join our email lists: Sign up
to get topic specific email
announcements or new
books, conferences, special
offers and technology news
elists.oreilly.com

For book content
technical questions:
booktech@oreilly.com

To submit new book
proposals to our editors:
proposals@oreilly.com

Contact us:
O'Reilly Media, Inc.
1005 Gravenstein Highway N.
Sebastopol, CA U.S.A. 95472
707-827-7000 or
800-998-9938
www.oreilly.com

Did you know that if you register
your O'Reilly books, you'll get
automatic notification and upgrade
discounts on new editions?

**And that's not all! Once you've registered
your books you can:**

» Win free books, T-shirts and O'Reilly Gear

» Get special offers available only to registered
O'Reilly customers

» Get free catalogs announcing all our new
titles (US and UK Only)

**Registering is easy! Just go to
www.oreilly.com/go/register**

O'REILLY®

Try the online edition
free for 45 days

The Art of Lean
Software Development

O'REILLY®   Curt Hibbs, Steve Jewett & Mike Sullivan

Get the information you need when you need it, with Safari Books Online. Safari
Books Online contains the complete version of the print book in your hands plus
thousands of titles from the best technical publishers, with sample code ready to
cut and paste into your applications.

Safari is designed for people in a hurry to get the answers they need so they can
get the job done. You can find what you need in the morning, and put it to work in
the afternoon. As simple as cut, paste, and program.

**To try out Safari and the online edition of the above title FREE for 45 days,
go to www.oreilly.com/go/safarienabled and enter the coupon code MPIQYCB.**

To see the complete Safari Library visit:
safari.oreilly.com

70502